Great Recitations

Great Recitations

Compiled By
Sanford W. Jones

HART PUBLISHING COMPANY, INC.

NEW YORK CITY

ACKNOWLEDGMENTS

"The Cremation of Sam McGee," "The Shooting of Dan McGrew," "Jean Desprez," and "Fleurette" are reprinted by permission of Dodd, Mead & Company, Inc. from *The Collected Poems of Robert Service.* Copyright 1907, 1909, 1912, 1916, 1921 by Dodd, Mead & Company, Inc. Copyright renewed 1935, 1937, 1940, 1944, 1949 by Robert W. Service.

THE PUBLISHER HAS MADE EVERY EFFORT TO SECURE PERMISSION FROM OWNERS OF COPYRIGHT. IF THROUGH SOME UNKNOWING OMISSION SUCH PERMISSION HAS NOT BEEN OBTAINED, FORGIVENESS IS ASKED.

Contents

The Face
on the Barroom Floor

JOHN HENRY TITUS (1853-1947)

'Twas a balmy summer evening, and a goodly crowd
    was there,
Which well-nigh filled Joe's barroom on the corner of
    the square,
And as songs and witty stories came through the open
    door
A vagabond crept slowly in and posed upon the
    floor.

"Where did it come from?" someone said: "The wind
    has blown it in."
"What does it want?" another cried. "Some whisky,
    rum or gin?"
"Here, Toby, seek him, if your stomach's equal to the
    work—
I wouldn't touch him with a fork, he's as filthy as a
    Turk."

This badinage the poor wretch took with stoical
    good grace;
In fact, he smiled as though he thought he'd struck
    the proper place.

7

"Come, boys, I know there's kindly hearts among so
    good a crowd—
To be in such good company would make a deacon
    proud.

"Give me a drink—that's what I want—I'm out of
    funds, you know;
When I had cash to treat the gang, this hand was
    never slow.
What? You laugh as though you thought this pocket
    never held a sou;
I once was fixed as well, my boys, as anyone of you.

"There, thanks; that's braced me nicely; God bless
    you one and all;
Next time I pass this good saloon, I'll make another
    call.
Give you a song? No, I can't do that, my singing days
    are past;
My voice is cracked, my throat's worn out, and my
    lungs are going fast.

"Say! Give me another whisky, and I'll tell you what
    I'll do—
I'll tell you a funny story, and a fact, I promise, too.
That I was ever a decent man not one of you would
    think;
But I was, some four or five years back. Say, give me
    another drink.

"Fill her up, Joe, I want to put some lift into my
     frame—
Such little drinks, to a bum like me, are miserably
     tame;
Five fingers—there, that's the scheme—and corking
     whisky, too.
Well, here's luck, boys; and, landlord, my best
     regards to you.

"You've treated me pretty kindly, and I'd like to tell
     you how
I came to be the dirty sot you see before you now.
As I told you, once I was a man, with muscle, frame
     and health,
And, but for a blunder, ought to have made
     considerable wealth.

"I was a painter—not one that daubed on bricks and
     wood
But an artist, and, for my age, was rated pretty good.
I worked hard at my canvas and was bidding fair to
     rise,
For gradually I saw the star of fame before my eyes.

"I made a picture, perhaps you've seen, 'tis called the
     'Chase of Fame.'
It brought me a thousand dollars and added to my
     name.

And then I met a woman—now comes the funny
     part—
With eyes that petrified my brain, and sank into my
     heart.

"Why don't you laugh? 'Tis funny that the vagabond
     you see
Could ever love a woman and expect her love for me;
But for two blessed months and more her smiles were
     freely given,
And when her loving lips touched mine it carried me
     to heaven.

"Say, boys, did you ever see a woman for whom your
     soul you'd give,
With a form like the Milo Venus, too beautiful to live;

With eyes that would beat the Koh-i-noor, and a
    wealth of chestnut hair?
If so, 'twas she, for no one else was ever half so fair.

"I was working on a portrait, one afternoon in May,
Of a fair-haired boy, a friend of mine, who lived
    across the way,
And Madeline admired it, and much to my surprise,
Said she'd like to know the man that had such dreamy
    eyes.

"It didn't take long to know him, and before the
    month had flown
My friend had stole' my darling, and I was left alone;
And, ere a year of misery had passed above my head,
This aching, breaking heart of mine had withered
    and was dead.

"That's why I took to drink, boys. Why, I never saw
    you smile,
I thought you'd be amused, and laughing all the
    while.
Why, what's the matter, friend? There's a teardrop in
    your eye,
Come, laugh, like me; 'tis women that should cry.

"Say, boys, give me another whisky, and that will
    make me glad,
And I'll draw right here a picture of the face that
    drove me mad.

Hand me, please, that chalk with which you mark the
    baseball score—
You'll see the lovely Madeline upon this barroom
    floor."

Another drink, and with chalk in hand the vagabond
    began
To sketch a face that well might buy the soul of any
    man.
Then, as he placed another lock upon the shapely
    head,
With fearful shriek, he leaped and fell across the
    picture—dead.

*John Henry Titus is, in a sense, co-author of this
ballad with Hugh Antoine D'Arcy, a noted actor of
the 1880's. Titus's version of the poem, titled "The
Face upon the Floor" was published in the* Sentinel *of
Ashtabula, Ohio, in 1872. It seems that D'Arcy
subsequently made the piece a part of his oratorical
repertoire, changing it substantially in the process.
When the poem next appeared in print, in an edition
of the New York* Dispatch *of 1887, D'Arcy was
credited as the author. The version above is the one
improved by D'Arcy.*

*"The Face on the Barroom Floor" was the most
popular American recitation of its day, and it remains
a grand old warhorse. By the way, the "Joe's
barroom" of the poem is "Joe's" of Union Square in
New York, long since departed.*

Lochinvar

SIR WALTER SCOTT (1771-1832)

Oh! young Lochinvar is come out of the West,
Through all the wide Border his steed was the best,
And save his good broadsword he weapon had
    none,—
He rode all unarm'd and he rode all alone.
So faithful in love, and so dauntless in war,
There never was knight like the young Lochinvar.

He stay'd not for brake, and he stopp'd not for stone,
He swam the Eske river where ford there was none,
But ere he alighted at Netherby gate,
The bride had consented, the gallant came late;
For a laggard in love and a dastard in war
Was to wed the fair Ellen of brave Lochinvar.

So boldly he enter'd the Netherby hall,
'Mong bridesmen and kinsmen and brothers and all.
Then spoke the bride's father, his hand on his sword
(For the poor craven bridegroom said never a word),
"Oh, come ye in peace here, or come ye in war,
Or to dance at our bridal, young Lord Lochinvar?"

"I long woo'd your daughter,—my suit you denied;
Love swells like the Solway, but ebbs like its tide;

And now am I come, with this lost love of mine
To lead but one measure, drink one cup of wine.
There are maidens in Scotland more lovely, by far,
That would gladly be bride to the young Lochinvar."

The bride kissed the goblet, the knight took it up,
He quaff'd at the wine and he threw down the cup.
She look'd down to blush, and she look'd up to sigh,
With a smile on her lips and a tear in her eye.
He took her soft hand ere her mother could bar:
"Now tread we a measure," said young Lochinvar.

So stately his form, and so lovely her face,
That never a hall such a galliard did grace,
While her mother did fret, and her father did fume,
And the bridegroom stood dangling his bonnet and
    plume,
And the bridesmaidens whisper'd, "'Twere better by
    far
To have match'd our fair cousin with young Lochin-
    var."

One touch to her hand, and one word in her ear,
When they reach'd the hall-door, and the charger
    stood near;
So light to the croupe the fair lady he swung,
So light to the saddle before her he sprung!

"She is won! we are gone, over bank, bush, and scaur;
They'll have fleet steeds that follow," quoth young
    Lochinvar.

There was mounting 'mong Graemes of the Netherby
    clan;
Forsters, Fenwicks, and Musgraves, they rode and
    they ran;
There was racing and chasing on Cannobie Lee,
But the lost bride of Netherby ne'er did they see.
So daring in love, and so dauntless in war,
Have ye e'er heard of gallant like young Lochinvar?

Sir Walter Scott was born and educated in Edinburgh, and made his initial literary mark with his Minstrelsy of the Scottish Border *(1802), a scholarly collection of old ballads. This was followed by his first major poem,* The Lay of the Last Minstrel *(1805), and* Marmion *(1808), of which "Lochinvar" is the fifth canto.*

After The Lady of the Lake *(1810), Scott embarked upon the long string of historical novels and romances which made his fortune—*Waverly, The Heart of Midlothian, Ivanhoe, Kenilworth, Quentin Durward, *etc. Like Mark Twain decades later, Scott was financially ruined by his decision to publish his own books. Rather than declare his firm bankrupt, Scott attempted to liquidate his enormous debt by churning out more novels. This feverish activity led to collapse, and, after a belated rest cure in Italy, death at his famed Abbotsford estate.*

Blow Me Eyes

WALLACE IRWIN (1876-1959)

When I was young and full o' pride,
   A-standin' on the grass
And gazin' o'er the water-side,
   I seen a fisher lass.
"O, fisher lass, be kind awhile,"
   I asks 'er quite unbid.
"Please look into me face and smile"—
   And, blow me eyes, she did!

     O, blow me light and blow me blow,
     I didn't think she'd charm me so—
       But, blow me eyes, she did!

She seemed so young and beautiful
   I *had* to speak perlite,
(The afternoon was long and dull,
   But she was short and bright).
"This ain't no place," I says, "to stand—
   Let's take a walk instid,
Each holdin' of the other's hand"—
   And, blow me eyes, she did!

     O, blow me light and blow me blow,
     I sort o' thunk she wouldn't go—
       But, blow me eyes, she did!

And as we walked along a lane
   With no one else to see,
Me heart was filled with sudden pain,
   And so I says to she:
"If you would have me actions speak
   The words what can't be hid,
You'd sort o' let me kiss yer cheek"—
   And, blow me eyes, she did!

      O, blow me light and blow me blow,
      How sweet she was I didn't know—
         But, blow me eyes, *she* did!

But pretty soon me shipmate Jim
   Came strollin' down the beach,
And she began a-oglin' him
   As pretty as a peach.
"O, fickle maid o' false intent,"
   Impulsively I chid,
"Why don't you go and wed that gent?"
   And, blow me eyes, she did!

      O, blow me light and blow me blow,
      I didn't think she'd treat me so—
         But, blow me eyes, she did!

Wallace Irwin was born in Oneida, New York, and went west to Stanford for his education. After graduating in 1899, he hooked up with William Randolph Hearst's San Francisco Examiner, *which he served as a local reporter and foreign correspondent. In 1902, he became editor of the* Overland Monthly, *and for many years thereafter, he also wrote for* Collier's. *Irwin is perhaps best known for his* Love Sonnets of a Hoodlum *(1902) and* Letters of a Japanese Schoolboy *(1903).*

"Blow Me Eyes" is written in the form of a sea chantey, with its great rollicking rhythm. As in most chanteys, the wind is a prominent image, here inflating the ardor of the seaman and then letting it go slack. Likewise, the fisher lass blows hot and cold, as fickle as the wind.

Casabianca

FELICIA HEMANS (1793-1835)

The boy stood on the burning deck,
    Whence all but him had fled;
The flame that lit the battle's wreck
    Shone round him o'er the dead.

Yet beautiful and bright he stood,
    As born to rule the storm;
A creature of heroic blood,
    A proud though childlike form.

The flames rolled on; he would not go
    Without his father's word;
That father, faint in death below,
    His voice no longer heard.

He called aloud, "Say, Father, say,
    If yet my task be done!"
He knew not that the chieftain lay
    Unconscious of his son.

"Speak, Father!" once again he cried,
    "If I may yet be gone!"
And but the booming shots replied,
    And fast the flames rolled on.

Upon his brow he felt their breath,
  And in his waving hair,
And looked from that lone post of death
  In still yet brave despair;

And shouted but once more aloud,
  "My father! must I stay?"
While o'er him fast, through sail and shroud,
  The wreathing fires made way.

They wrapt the ship in splendor wild,
  They caught the flag on high,
And streamed above the gallant child,
  Like banners in the sky.

There came a burst of thunder sound;
    The boy,—Oh! where was *he?*
Ask of the winds, that far around
    With fragments strewed the sea,—

With shroud and mast and pennon fair,
    That well had borne their part,—
But the noblest thing that perished there
    Was that young, faithful heart.

Felicia Dorothea Hemans née Browne is today remembered, if at all, for three poems— "Casabianca" (better known by its first line, "The boy stood on the burning deck"), "The Landing of the Pilgrim Fathers in New England," and "England's Dead." Yet in her day, Mrs. Hemans was counted as the equal of Shelley, Scott, Wordsworth, and Byron—by those poets, as well as by her reading public.

Louis de Casabianca, father of the boy hero of the poem, commanded the French ship L'Orient in the Battle of the Nile in 1798. The boy, thirteen years old, did indeed stand on the deck after all the crew had died or abandoned ship. He perished when the flames reached the powder stored below.

The Shooting of Dan McGrew

ROBERT SERVICE· (1874-1958)

A bunch of the boys were whooping it up in the
    Malamute saloon;
The kid that handles the music-box was hitting a rag-
    time tune;
Back of the bar, in a solo game, sat Dangerous Dan
    McGrew,
And watching his luck was his light-o'-love, the lady
    that's known as Lou.

When out of the night, which was fifty below, and
     into the din and the glare,
There stumbled a miner fresh from the creeks, dog-
     dirty, and loaded for bear.
He looked like a man with a foot in the grave and
     scarcely the strength of a louse,
Yet he tilted a poke of dust on the bar, and he called
     for drinks for the house.
There was none could place the stranger's face,
     though we searched ourselves for a clue;
But we drank his health, and the last to drink was
     Dangerous Dan McGrew.

There's men that somehow just grip your eyes, and
     hold them hard like a spell;
And such was he, and he looked to me like a man who
     had lived in hell;
With a face most hair, and the dreary stare of a dog
     whose day is done,
As he watered the green stuff in his glass, and the
     drops fell one by one.
Then I got to figgering who he was, and wondering
     what he'd do,
And I turned my head—and there watching him was
     the lady that's known as Lou.

His eyes went rubbering round the room, and he
     seemed in a kind of daze,
Till at last that old piano fell in the way of his
     wandering gaze.

The rag-time kid was having a drink; there was no
    one else on the stool,
So the stranger stumbles across the room, and flops
    down there like a fool.
In a buckskin shirt that was glazed with dirt he sat,
    and I saw him sway;
Then he clutched the keys with his talon hands—my
    God! but that man could play.

Were you ever out in the Great Alone, when the
    moon was awful clear,
And the icy mountains hemmed you in with a silence
    you most could *hear;*
With only the howl of a timber wolf, and you
    camped there in the cold,
A half-dead thing in a stark, dead world, clean mad
    for the muck called gold;
While high overhead, green, yellow and red, the
    North Lights swept in bars?—
Then you've a hunch what the music meant . . .
    hunger and night and the stars.

And hunger not of the belly kind, that's banished
    with bacon and beans,
But the gnawing hunger of lonely men for a home
    and all that it means;
For a fireside far from the cares that are, four walls
    and a roof above;
But oh! so cramful of cosy joy, and crowned with a
    woman's love—

A woman dearer than all the world, and true as
    Heaven is true—
(God! how ghastly she looks through her rouge,—the
    lady that's known as Lou.)

Then on a sudden the music changed, so soft that you
    scarce could hear;
But you felt that your life had been looted clean of all
    that it once held dear;
That someone had stolen the woman you loved; that
    her love was a devil's lie;
That your guts were gone, and the best for you was to
    crawl away and die.
'Twas the crowning cry of a heart's despair, and it
    thrilled you through and through—
"I guess I'll make it a spread misere," said Dangerous
    Dan McGrew.

The music almost died away . . . then it burst like a
    pent-up flood;
And it seemed to say, "Repay, repay," and my eyes
    were blind with blood.
The thought came back of an ancient wrong, and it
    stung like a frozen lash,
And the lust awoke to kill, to kill . . . then the music
    stopped with a crash,
And the stranger turned, and his eyes they burned in
    a most peculiar way;

In a buckskin shirt that was glazed with dirt he sat,
    and I saw him sway;

Then his lips went in in a kind of grin, and he spoke,
and his voice was calm,
And "Boys," says he, "you don't know me, and none
of you care a damn;
But I want to state, and my words are straight, and I'll
bet my poke they're true,
That one of you is a hound of hell . . . and that one is
Dan McGrew."

Then I ducked my head, and the lights went out, and
two guns blazed in the dark,
And a woman screamed, and the lights went up, and
two men lay stiff and stark.
Pitched on his head, and pumped full of lead, was
Dangerous Dan McGrew,
While the man from the creeks lay clutched to the
breast of the lady that's known as Lou.

These are the simple facts of the case, and I guess I
    ought to know.
They say that the stranger was crazed with "hooch,"
    and I'm not denying it's so.
I'm not so wise as the lawyer guys, but strictly
    between us two—
The woman that kissed him and—pinched his
    poke—was the lady that's known as Lou.

*Robert William Service was born in Scotland and
educated at the University of Glasgow. At the age of
25, he went to western Canada where, among other
jobs, he worked for the Canadian Bank of Com-
merce. His experiences in British Columbia and the
Yukon were set down in verse in* Songs of a
Sourdough *(1907), later reprinted as* The Spell of the
Yukon. *"The Shooting of Dan McGrew" and "The
Cremation of Sam McGee" are two of the better-
known poems in that volume.*

*Service became a European foreign correspon-
dent in 1912, and when the War broke out, he
volunteered for the ambulance corps. His ex-
periences with the Red Cross led to his writing*
Rhymes of a Red Cross Man *(1916).*

*For the rest of his life, Service lived in France and
Monte Carlo, except during the German Occupation
in World War II. Those years he spent in the U. S.,
including a brief stay in Hollywood to observe the
filming of his life story.*

Life-Lesson

JAMES WHITCOMB RILEY (1849-1916)

There! little girl; don't cry!
  They have broken your doll, I know;
    And your tea-set blue,
    And your play-house, too,
  Are things of the long ago;
    But childish troubles will soon pass by
      There! little girl; don't cry!

There! little girl; don't cry!
  They have broken your slate, I know;
    And the glad, wild ways
    Of your school-girl days
  Are things of the long ago;
    But life and love will soon come by.
      There! little girl; don't cry!

There! little girl; don't cry!
　They have broken your heart, I know;
　　And the rainbow gleams
　　Of your youthful dreams
　Are things of the long ago;
　　But heaven holds all for which you sigh.
　　　There! little girl; don't cry!

James Whitcomb Riley took a crack at play-acting, sign-painting, and newspaper reporting before finding his calling as a poet. Under the pseudonym "Benjamin F. Johnson of Boone," Riley began writing verse for the Indianapolis Journal *in 1875. These poems appeared in book form eight years later, in* The Old Swimmin' Hole and 'Leven More. *Riley's homespun, folksy style—often in Hoosier dialect—caught on, and he soon was being called the "poet of the people" and the "Hoosier Burns."*

Riley's readings and lectures were extremely popular, for he was the consummate ham, and knew how to pluck the heartstrings of his audience. Like Dickens and Twain, he was a prince of the platform.

Among Riley's enduring poems are "Little Orphant Annie," "The Raggedy Man," "He Is Not Dead," and "The Runaway Boy." Though Riley received the barbs of the literati both during and after his lifetime, he remains a favorite among the common folk, the only people whose favor he courted.

Ostler Joe

GEORGE R. SIMS (1847-1922)

I stood at eve, as the sun went down, by a grave
    where a woman lies,
Who lured men's souls to the shores of sin with the
    light of her wanton eyes;
Who sang the song that the Siren sang on the
    treacherous Lurley height,
Whose face was as fair as a summer day, and whose
    heart was as black as night.

Yet a blossom I fain would pluck today from the
    garden above her dust—
Not the languorous lily of soulless sin, nor the blood-
    red rose of lust,

But a pure white blossom of holy love that grew in
the one green spot
In the arid desert of Phryne's life, where all was
parched and hot.

In the summer, when the meadows were aglow with
blue and red,
Joe, the hostler of the "Magpie," and fair Annie Smith
were wed.
Plump was Annie, plump and pretty, with cheek as
white as snow;
He was anything but handsome, was the "Magpie"
hostler, Joe.

But he won the winsome lassie. They'd a cottage and
a cow;
And her matronhood sat lightly on the village
beauty's brow.
Sped the months and came a baby—such a blue-eyed
baby boy;
Joe was working in the stables when they told him of
his joy.

He was rubbing down the horses, and he gave them
then and there
All a special feed of clover, just in honor of the heir.
It had been his great ambition, and he told the horses
so,
That the Fates would send a baby who might bear
the name of Joe.

Little Joe the child was christened, and, like babies,
   grew apace,
He'd his mother's eyes of azure and his father's
   honest face.
Swift the happy years went over, years of blue and
   cloudless sky;
Love was lord of that small cottage, and the tempest
   passed them by.

Passed them by for years, then swiftly burst in fury
   o'er their home.
Down the lane by Annie's cottage chanced a
   gentleman to roam;
Thrice he came and saw her sitting by the window
   with her child,
And he nodded to the baby, and the baby laughed
   and smiled.

So at last it grew to know him—little Joe was nearly
   four—
He would call the "pretty gemlum" as he passed the
   open door;
And one day he ran and caught him, and in child's
   play pulled him in,
And the baby Joe had prayed for brought about the
   mother's sin.

'Twas the same old wretched story that for ages
   bards had sung,
'Twas a woman weak and wanton, and a villain's
   tempting tongue;

'Twas a picture deftly painted for a silly creature's
　　eyes
Of the Babylonian wonders, and the joy that in them
　　lies.

Annie listened and was tempted—she was tempted
　　and she fell,
As the angel fell from heaven to the blackest depths
　　of hell;
She was promised wealth and splendour, and a life of
　　guilty sloth,
Yellow gold for child and husband—and the woman
　　left them both.

Home one eve came Joe the hostler, with a cheery
　　cry of "Wife,"
Finding that which blurred forever all the story of his
　　life.
She had left a silly letter,—through the cruel scrawl
　　he spelt;
Then he sought his lonely bedroom, joined his horny
　　hands, and knelt.

"Now, O Lord, O God, forgive her, for she ain't to
　　blame," he cried;
"For I owt to seen her trouble, and 'a' gone away and
　　died.
Why, a wench like her—God bless her! 'twasn't likely
　　as her'd rest
With that bonnie head forever on a hostler's rugged
　　breast.

"It was kind o' her to bear me all this long and happy
     time;
So, for my sake please to bless her, though you count
     her deed a crime;
If so be I don't pray proper, Lord, forgive me; for
     you see
I can talk all right to 'osses; but I'm nervouslike with
     Thee."

Ne'er a line came to the cottage, from the woman
     who had flown;
Joe, the baby, died that winter, and the man was left
     alone.
Ne'er a bitter word he uttered, but in silence kissed
     the rod,
Saving what he told the horses—saving what he told
     his God.

Far away, in mighty London, rose the woman into
     fame,
For her beauty won men's homage, and she
     prospered in her shame.
Quick from lord to lord she flitted, higher still each
     prize she won,
And her rivals paled beside her, as the stars beside the
     sun.

Next she trod the stage half naked, and she dragged a
     temple down
To the level of a market for the women of the town.

And the kisses she had given to poor hostler Joe for
     naught
With their gold and priceless jewels rich and titled
     roués bought.

Went the years with flying footsteps while her star
     was at its height,
Then the darkness came on swiftly, and the gloaming
     turned to night.
Shattered strength and faded beauty tore the laurels
     from her brow;
Of the thousands who had worshipped never one
     came near her now.

Broken down in health and fortune, men forgot her
     very name,
Till the news that she was dying woke the echoes of
     her fame;

And the papers, in their gossip, mentioned how an
    actress lay
Sick to death in humble lodgings, growing weaker
    every day.

One there was who read the story in a far-off country
    place,
And that night the dying woman woke and looked
    upon his face.
Once again the strong arms clasped her that had
    clasped her years ago,
And the weary head lay pillowed on the breast of
    hostler Joe.

All the past had he forgiven, all the sorrow and the
    shame;
He had found her sick and lonely, and his wife he
    now could claim,
Since the grand folks who had known her, one and
    all, had slunk away,
He could clasp his long-lost darling, and no man
    would say him nay.

In his arms death found her lying, in his arms her
    spirit fled;
And his tears came down in torrents as he knelt
    beside her dead.
Never once his love had faltered, through her base,
    unhallowed life,
And the stone above her ashes bears the honored
    name of wife.

That's the blossom I fain would pluck today, from
    the garden above her dust;
Not the languorous lily of soulless sin, nor the blood-
    red rose of lust;
But a sweet white blossom of holy love, that grew in
    the one green spot
In the arid desert of Phryne's life, where all was
    parched and hot.

*George Robert Sims suffered perhaps the most
meteoric plummet from fame of any poet in this
volume. Less than a hundred years ago, one
Victorian anthologist included Sims among the
"dozen grand and noble poets of humanity," with
such as Burns, Wordsworth, and Longfellow. Today,
even his most popular poems—"Ostler Joe," "The
Lifeboat," and "In the Workhouse: Christmas
Day"—are scarcely known.*

*"Ostler Joe" tells the story of the stableman of the
Magpie Inn and his Phryne-like wife (Phryne was the
Greek courtesan who, charged with impiety, was
acquitted when her nude form was displayed for the
court). The poem was written for the actor Edmund
Yates, and is said to have been read by four-fifths of
American adults within a few years of its
appearance.*

*Sims was also a famous journalist, playwright,
novelist, and social reformer. One of his lesser but
intriguing accomplishments is the hair restorer he
patented—"Tatcho," named for his publisher, Mr.
Chatto of Chatto & Windus.*

The Highwayman

ALFRED NOYES (1880-1958)

Part One

The wind was a torrent of darkness among the gusty
     trees,
The moon was a ghostly galleon tossed upon cloudy
     seas,
The road was a ribbon of moonlight over the purple
     moor,
And the highwayman came riding—
     Riding—riding—
The highwayman came riding, up to the old inn-
     door.

He'd a French cocked-hat on his forehead, a bunch
     of lace at his chin,
A coat of claret velvet, and breeches of brown
     doeskin:
They fitted with never a wrinkle; his boots were up to
     the thigh!
And he rode with a jewelled twinkle,
     His pistol butts a-twinkle,
His rapier hilt a-twinkle, under the jewelled sky.

Over the cobbles he clattered and clashed in the dark
    inn-yard,
And he tapped with his whip on the shutters, but all
    was locked and barred:
He whistled a tune to the window, and who should
    be waiting there
But the landlord's black-eyed daughter,
       Bess, the landlord's daughter,
Plaiting a dark red love-knot into her long black hair.

And then in the dark old inn-yard a stable-wicket
    creaked
Where Tim, the ostler, listened; his face was white
    and peaked,
His eyes were hollows of madness, his hair like
    moldy hay;
But he loved the landlord's daughter,
       The landlord's red-lipped daughter:
Dumb as a dog he listened, and he heard the robber
    say—

"One kiss, my bonny sweetheart, I'm after a prize
    tonight,
But I shall be back with the yellow gold before the
    morning light.
Yet if they press me sharply, and harry me through
    the day,
Then look for me by moonlight,
       Watch for me by moonlight:
I'll come to thee by moonlight, though Hell should
    bar the way."

He rose upright in the stirrups, he scarce could reach
her hand;
But she loosened her hair i' the casement! His face
burnt like a brand
As the black cascade of perfume came tumbling over
his breast;
And he kissed its waves in the moonlight,
      (Oh, sweet black waves in the moonlight)
Then he tugged at his reins in the moonlight, and
galloped away to the West.

Part Two

He did not come in the dawning; he did not come at
noon;
And out of the tawny sunset, before the rise o' the
moon,
When the road was a gypsy's ribbon, looping the
purple moor,
A red-coat troop came marching—
      Marching—marching—
King George's men came marching, up to the old inn-
door.

They said no word to the landlord, they drank his ale
    instead;
But they gagged his daughter and bound her to the
    foot of her narrow bed.
Two of them knelt at her casement, with muskets at
    the side!
There was death at every window;
        And Hell at one dark window;
For Bess could see, through her casement, the road
    that *he* would ride.

They had tied her up to attention, with many a
    sniggering jest:
They had bound a musket beside her, with the barrel
    beneath her breast!
"Now keep good watch!" and they kissed her.
        She heard the dead man say—
Look for me by moonlight;
        Watch for me by moonlight;
*I'll come to thee by moonlight, though Hell should
    bar the way!*

She twisted her hands behind her; but all the knots
    held good!
She writhed her hands till her fingers were wet with
    sweat or blood!
They stretched and strained in the darkness, and the
    hours crawled by like years;
Till, now, on the stroke of midnight,
        Cold, on the stroke of midnight,
The tip of one finger touched it! The trigger at least
    was hers!

The tip of one finger touched it; she strove no more
for the rest!
Up, she stood up to attention, with the barrel beneath
her breast,
She would not risk their hearing: she would not strive
again;
For the road lay bare in the moonlight,
        Blank and bare in the moonlight;
And the blood of her veins in the moonlight throbbed
to her Love's refrain.

Tlot-tlot, tlot-tlot! Had they heard it? The horse-
hoofs ringing clear—
Tlot-tlot, tlot-tlot, in the distance? Were they deaf
that they did not hear?
Down the ribbon of moonlight, over the brow of the
hill,
The highwayman came riding,
        Riding, riding!
The red-coats looked to their priming! She stood up
straight and still!

Tlot-tlot, in the frosty silence; *Tlot-tlot* in the echoing
night!
Nearer he came and nearer! Her face was like a light!
Her eyes grew wide for a moment; she drew one last
deep breath,
Then her finger moved in the moonlight,
        Her musket shattered the moonlight,
Shattered her breast in the moonlight and warned
him—with her death.

He turned; he spurred him Westward; he did not
    know who stood
Bowed with her head o'er the musket, drenched with
    her own red blood!
Not till the dawn he heard it, and slowly blanched to
    hear
How Bess, the landlord's daughter,
        The landlord's black-eyed daughter,
Had watched for her Love in the moonlight; and died
    in the darkness there.

Back, he spurred like a madman, shrieking a curse to
    the sky,
With the white road smoking behind him, and his
    rapier brandished high!
Blood-red were his spurs i' the golden noon; wine-red
    was his velvet coat;
When they shot him down on the highway,
        Down like a dog on the highway,
And he lay in his blood on the highway, with the
    bunch of lace at his throat.

*And still a winter's night, they say, when the wind is
    in the trees,*
*When the moon is a ghostly galleon tossed upon
    cloudy seas,*
*When the road is a ribbon of moonlight over the
    purple moor,*
A highwayman comes riding—
        Riding—riding—
A highwayman comes riding, up to the old inn-door.

*Over the cobbles he clatters and clangs in the dark
      inn-yard;*
*And he taps with his whip on the shutters, but all is
      locked and barred:*
*He whistles a tune to the window, and who should be
      waiting there*
But the landlord's black-eyed daughter,
            Bess, the landlord's daughter,
Plaiting a dark red love-knot into her long black hair.

Alfred Noyes, though a contemporary of such
modernists as T. S. Eliot, Ezra Pound, and Arthur
Symons, employed the verse conventions of the mid-
19th century. A staunch literary conservative, he
practiced the virtues of narrative as well as the
narrative of virtue. "The Highwayman" is one of his
finest heroic ballads.

Noyes was one of the few poets of his day who earned a solid living through sales of his poetry. Though born and bred in England, he came to the United States in 1913 with his American bride, and for ten years he lectured at Harvard and then Princeton. Some of his notable poems are "The Paradox," "The Loom of Years," "Sherwood," and "On Rembrandt's Portrait of a Rabbi."

Casey at the Bat

ERNEST L. THAYER (1863-1940)

The outlook wasn't brilliant for the Mudville nine
    that day,
The score stood two to four with just one inning left
    to play;
And so, when Cooney died at first, and Burrows did
    the same,
A sickly silence fell upon the patrons of the game.

A straggling few got up to go in deep despair. The
    rest
Clung to the hope that springs eternal within each
    human breast;
They thought if only Casey could but get a whack at
    that—
They'd put up *even money* now, with Casey at the
    bat.

But Flynn preceded Casey, and so did Jimmy Blake,
And the former was a washout, and the latter was a
    fake;
So upon that stricken multitude grim melancholy sat,
For there seemed but little chance of Casey's getting
    to the bat.

But Flynn let drive a single to the wonderment of all,
And Blake whom all had sneered at, tore the cover
    off the ball;

And when the dust had lifted, and they saw what had
    occurred,
There was Jimmy safe on second and Flynn a -
    huggin' third!

Then from the gladdened multitude went up a
    joyous yell,
It rumbled in the mountaintops, it rattled in the dell,
It struck upon the hillside and rebounded on the flat;
For Casey, mighty Casey, was advancing to the bat.

There was ease in Casey's manner as he stepped into
    his place,
There was pride in Casey's bearing, and a smile on
    Casey's face;

And when, responding to the cheers, he lightly
    doffed his hat,
No stranger in the crowd could doubt 'twas Casey at
    the bat.

Ten thousand eyes were upon him as he rubbed his
    hands with dirt;
Five thousand tongues applauded when he wiped
    them on his shirt.
Then while the writhing pitcher ground the ball into
    his hip,
Defiance gleamed in Casey's eye, a sneer curled
    Casey's lip.

And now the leather-covered sphere came hurtling
    through the air,
And Casey stood a-watching it in haughty grandeur
    there;
Close by the sturdy batsman the ball unheeded sped:
"That ain't my style," said Casey. "Strike one!" the
    umpire said.

From the benches, black with people, there went up
    a muffled roar,
Like the beating of the storm-waves on a stern and
    distant shore;
"Kill him! Kill the umpire!" shouted someone in the
    stands.
And it's sure they would have killed him had not
    Casey raised his hand.

With a smile of Christian charity great Casey's visage
    shone;
He stilled the rising tumult; he bade the game go on;
He signaled to the pitcher, and once more the
    spheroid flew,
But Casey still ignored it; and the umpire said, "Strike
    two!"

"Fraud!" cried the maddened thousands, and the
    echo answered "Fraud!"
But one scornful look from Casey and the audience
    was awed;
They saw his face grow stern and cold, they saw his
    muscles strain.
And they knew that Casey wouldn't let that ball go
    by again.

The sneer is gone from Casey's lip, his teeth are
    clenched with hate;
He pounds with cruel violence his bat upon the plate;
And now the pitcher holds the ball, and now he lets it
    go.
And now the air is shattered by the force of Casey's
    blow.

Oh, somewhere in this favored land the sun is shining
    bright;
The band is playing somewhere, and somewhere
    hearts are light;

And somewhere men are laughing, and somewhere
    children shout;
But there is no joy in Mudville—*mighty Casey has
    struck out!*

*Ernest Lawrence Thayer was born into a well-to-do
family in Lawrence, Massachusetts. As was expected
of him, he went to Harvard where he majored in
philosophy. However, he met a lad named William
Randolph Hearst who persuaded Thayer to write a
humor column for the San Francisco Examiner,
which the senior Hearst had just bought for young
Willie. Between 1886 and 1888, Thayer sent Hearst a
ballad every other week or so. His final ballad*

appeared on June 3, 1888. It was entitled "Casey at the Bat."

"Casey" was met with no great acclaim until a year later, when actor DeWolf Hopper recited it at Wallack's Theatre in New York, before an audience which included members of the Chicago White Sox and the New York Giants. It brought the house down, and still does. Hopper went on to recite it more than 10,000 times. "Casey" became the subject of a popular song, several silent movies, a Disney cartoon, and an operetta!

Casey's Revenge

GRANTLAND RICE (1880-1954)

There were saddened hearts in Mudville for a week
    or even more;
There were muttered oaths and curses—every fan in
    town was sore.
"Just think," said one, "how soft it looked with Casey
    at the bat,
And then to think he'd go and spring a bush league
    trick like that!"

All his past fame was forgotten—he was now a
    hopeless "shine."
They called him "Strike-Out Casey," from the mayor
    down the line;
And as he came to bat each day his bosom heaved a
    sigh,
While a look of hopeless fury shone in mighty Casey's
    eye.

He pondered in the days gone by that he had been
    their king,
That when he strolled up to the plate they made the
    welkin ring;
But now his nerve had vanished, for when he heard
    them hoot
He "fanned" or "popped out" daily, like some minor
    league recruit.

He soon began to sulk and loaf, his batting eye went
lame;
No home runs on the score card now were chalked
against his name;
The fans without exception gave the manager no
peace,
For one and all kept clamoring for Casey's quick
release.

The Mudville squad began to slump, the team was in
the air;
Their playing went from bad to worse—nobody
seemed to care.
"Back to the woods with Casey!" was the cry from
Rooters' Row.
"Get some one who can hit the ball, and let that big
dub go!"

The lane is long, some one has said, that never turns
again,
And Fate, though fickle, often gives another chance
to men;
And Casey smiled; his rugged face no longer wore a
frown—
The pitcher who had started all the trouble came to
town.

All Mudville had assembled—ten thousand fans had
come
To see the twirler who had put big Casey on the bum;

And when he stepped into the box, the multitude
    went wild;
He doffed his cap in proud disdain, but Casey only
    smiled.

"Play ball!" the umpire's voice rang out, and then the
    game began.
But in that throng of thousands there was not a single
    fan
Who thought that Mudville had a chance, and with
    the setting sun
Their hopes sank low—the rival team was leading
    "four to one."

The last half of the ninth came round, with no change
    in the score;
But when the first man up hit safe, the crowd began
    to roar;
The din increased, the echo of ten thousand shouts
    was heard
When the pitcher hit the second and gave "four balls"
    to the third.

Three men on base—nobody out—three runs to tie
    the game!
A triple meant the highest niche in Mudville's hall of
    fame;
But here the rally ended and the gloom was deep as
    night,
When the fourth one "fouled to catcher" and the fifth
    "flew out to right."

A dismal groan in chorus came; a scowl was on each
    face
When Casey walked up, bat in hand, and slowly took
    his place;
His bloodshot eyes in fury gleamed, his teeth were
    clenched in hate;
He gave his cap a vicious hook and pounded on the
    plate.

But fame is fleeting as the wind and glory fades
    away;
There were no wild and woolly cheers, no glad
    acclaim this day;
They hissed and groaned and hooted as they
    clamored: "Strike him out!"
But Casey gave no outward sign that he had heard
    this shout.

The pitcher smiled and cut one loose—across the
     plate it sped;
Another hiss, another groan. "Strike one!" the umpire
     said.
Zip! Like a shot the second curve broke just below
     the knee.
"Strike two!" the umpire roared aloud; but Casey
     made no plea.

No roasting for the umpire now—his was an easy lot;
But here the pitcher whirled again—was that a rifle
     shot?
A whack, a crack, and out through the space the
     leather pellet flew,
A blot against the distant sky, a speck against the
     blue.

Above the fence in center field in rapid whirling
     flight
The sphere sailed on—the blot grew dim and then
     was lost to sight.
Ten thousand hats were thrown in air, ten thousand
     threw a fit,
But no one ever found the ball that mighty Casey hit.

O, somewhere in this favored land dark clouds may
     hide the sun,

And somewhere bands no longer play and children
    have no fun!
And somewhere over blighted lives there hangs a
    heavy pall,
But Mudville hearts are happy now, *for Casey hit the
    ball.*

*Grantland Rice was recognized as the best
sportswriter of his day, as well as the most prolific.
From the day he joined the Nashville* News *in 1901
until his death, he committed more than 60 million
words to paper! In addition to his sports columns for
the Nashville* Tennesseean, *the New York* Tribune,
*and hundreds of other papers through syndication,
Rice wrote several books:* Base-Ball Ballads *(1910),*
Songs of the Stalwart *(1917),* Songs of the Open
(1924), Only the Brave *(1941), and* The Tumult and
the Shouting *(1954).*

    *"Casey's Revenge" was written in 1906, and has
most often been attributed to one James Wilson—
Rice's early pseudonym.*

Casey—Twenty Years Later

CLARENCE PATRICK McDONALD

The Mudville Team was desperate in that big
    championship game;
The chances were they'd bite the dust and kiss
    goodbye to Fame;
Three men were hurt and two were benched; the
    score stood six to four.
They had to make three big, big runs in just two
    innings more.

"It can't be done," the captain said, a pallor on his
    face;
"I've got two has-beens in the field, a jerk on second
    base;
And should another man get spiked or crippled in
    some way,
The team could sure be counted out, with only eight
    to play.

"We're up against it anyhow, as far as I can see;
My boys ain't hitting like they should, and that's what
    worries me;
The luck's all with the other side; the pennant we
    can't win;
It's mighty tough! There's nought to do but take it on
    the chin."

The eighth round opened: one, two, three—the
enemy went down;
But Mudville went out quite the same. The captain
wore a frown.
The first half of the ninth came round, two men had
been called out,
When Mudville's catcher broke a thumb, and could
not go the route.

A deathly silence settled on the crowd assembled
there.
Defeat, defeat was what all sensed! Defeat hung in
the air!
With only eight men in the field, 'twould be a
gruesome fray;
Small wonder that the captain cursed the day he
learned to play.

"Lend me a man to finish with," he begged the other
team;
"Lend you a man?" the foe replied; "My boy, you're
in a dream!
We want that dear old pennant, pal." And then, a
final jeer—
"There's only one thing you can do—*call for a
volunteer.*"

The captain stood and pondered in a listless sort of
way;
He never was a quitter and wouldn't quit today.

"Is there within the grandstand here"—his voice rang
　　loud and clear—
"A man who has the sporting blood to be a
　　volunteer?"

A sense of death now settled o'er that sickly
　　multitude;
Was there a man among them with such recklessness
　　imbued?
The captain stood with cap in hand, and hopeless
　　was his glance, .
And then a big old man cried out, "Say, Cap, I'll take
　　a chance!"

Into the field he bounded with a step both firm and
　　light;
"Give me the mask and mitt," he said. "Let's get in
　　there and fight!
The game is not beyond recall; a winner you have
　　found;
Although I'm ancient, I'm a brute and muscular and
　　sound."

His hair was sprinkled here and there with little
　　streaks of gray;
Around his eyes and on his brow, a bunch of wrinkles
　　lay.
The captain smiled despairingly, and slowly turned
　　away.
"Why, he's all right," one rooter yelled. "C'mon, Cap,
　　let him play!"

"All right, go on," the captain sighed. The stranger
    turned around,
Took off his coat—and collar, too—and threw them
    on the ground.
The humor of the situation seemed to hit them one
    and all,
And as the stranger donned his mask, the umpire
    yelled, "Play ball!"

Three balls the pitcher at him hurled, three balls of
    lightning speed;
The oldster caught them all with ease and did not
    seem to heed.
Each ball had been pronounced a strike the side had
    been put out,
And as he walked in towards the bench, he heard the
    rooters shout.

One Mudville boy went out on strikes, and one was
    killed at first;
The captain saw his hopes all dashed, and gnashed
    his teeth and cursed.
But the next man smashed a double; and the fourth
    man swatted clear;
And in a thunder of applause, up came the volunteer.

His feet were planted in the earth, he swung a warlike
    club;
The captain saw his awkward pose, and softly
    whispered, "Dub!"
The pitcher looked at him and grinned, then heaved
    a speedy pill—
And the echo of that fearful swat, it lingers with us
    still.

High, fast and far that spheroid flew; it sailed and
    sailed away;
It ne'er was found, so it's supposed it still floats on
    today.
Three runs came in, the pennant would be Mudville's
    for a year;
The fans and players gathered round to cheer the
    volunteer.

"What is your name?" the captain asked. "Tell us
    your name!" cried all;
And down the unknown's cheeks great tears in
    rivulets did fall.

For one brief moment he was still, then murmured
　　soft and low:
"I'm mighty Casey who struck out—just twenty
　　years ago!"

Clarence Patrick McDonald is the mysterious author of this satisfying sequel to "Casey at the Bat." Nothing is known of his life except that he wrote at least one other poem—"Like Kelly Did," another in the Casey canon—and between 1918 and 1925, four little volumes of inspirational verse.

McDonald's ballad, like Grantland Rice's "Casey's Revenge," eases the frustration of anyone who has been pained at the last line of "Casey at the Bat." There are more than twenty "Casey" poems, including "Mrs. Casey at the Bat," "Casey's Son," "Casey's Sister at the Bat," "Casey's Daughter at the Bat," and, unbelievably, "Casey—Forty Years Later."

Abou Ben Adhem

LEIGH HUNT (1784-1859)

Abou Ben Adhem (may his tribe increase!)
Awoke one night from a deep dream of peace,
And saw, within the moonlight in his room,
Making it rich, and like a lily in bloom,
An Angel writing in a book of gold:
Exceeding peace had made Ben Adhem bold,
And to the Presence in the room he said,
"What writest thou?" The Vision raised its head,
And with a look made of all sweet accord
Answered, "The names of those who love the Lord."
"And is mine one?" said Abou. "Nay, not so,"
Replied the Angel. Abou spoke more low,
But cheerly still; and said, "I pray thee, then,
Write me as one that loves his fellow-men."

The Angel wrote, and vanished. The next night
It came again with a great wakening light,
And showed the names whom love of God had
    blessed,
And, lo! Ben Adhem's name led all the rest!

*James Henry Leigh Hunt was perhaps more
important for the influence he exerted on his
friends—Byron, Lamb, Shelley, Keats, Dickens—
than for his own creations. Of all the poems, novels,
articles, plays, and critiques he wrote, Hunt is little
read today except for the rondeau "Jenny Kissed
Me," and "Abou Ben Adhem," the fourteenth line of
which is inscribed on his tomb.*

*In 1808, with his brother John, he established a
liberal weekly called* The Examiner. *Five years later,
in that journal, Hunt's intemperate characterization
of the Prince Regent as "a fat Adonis of 50" and
"despiser of domestic ties" landed Hunt two years in
jail. There he was visited by Byron, Lamb, and others
who were to people his gossipy* Autobiography *of
1850. Some of the other journals Hunt managed or
wrote for were* The Morning Chronicle, The
Reflector, The Liberal, The Companion, *and* The
Tatler.

Beth Gêlert

WILLIAM ROBERT SPENCER (1769-1834)

The spearmen heard the bugle sound,
 And cheerily smiled the morn;
And many a brach, and many a hound
 Obeyed Llewellyn's horn.

And still he blew a louder blast,
 And gave a lustier cheer,
"Come, Gêlert, come, wert never last
 Llewellyn's horn to hear.

"O where does faithful Gêlert roam
 The flower of all his race;
So true, so brave—a lamb at home,
 A lion in the chase?"

In sooth, he was a peerless hound,
 The gift of royal John;
But now no Gêlert could be found,
 And all the chase rode on.

That day Llewellyn little loved
 The chase of hart and hare;
And scant and small the booty proved,
 For Gêlert was not there.

Unpleased, Llewellyn homeward hied,
    When, near the portal seat,
Hit truant Gêlert he espied
    Bounding his lord to greet.

But when he gained the castle-door,
    Aghast the chieftain stood;
The hound all o'er was smeared with gore;
    His lips, his fangs, ran blood.

Llewellyn gazed with fierce surprise;
    Unused such looks to meet,
His favorite checked his joyful guise,
    And crouched, and licked his feet.

Onward, in haste, Llewelyn passed,
    And on went Gêlert too;
And still, where'er his eyes he cast,
    Fresh blood-gouts shocked his view.

O'erturned his infant's bed he found,
    With blood-stained covert rent;
And all around the walls and ground
    With recent blood besprent.

He called his child—no voice replied—
He searched with terror wild
Blood, blood he found on every side,
    But nowhere found his child.

"Hell-hound! my child's by thee devoured,"
    The frantic father cried;
And to the hilt his vengeful sword
    He plunged in Gêlert's side.

Aroused by Gêlert's dying yell,
    Some slumberer wakened nigh;
What words the parent's joy could tell
    To hear his infant's cry!

Concealed beneath a tumbled heap
    His hurried search had missed,
All glowing from his rosy sleep
    The cherub boy he kissed.

Nor scathe had he, nor harm, nor dread,
    But, the same couch beneath,
Lay a gaunt wolf, all torn and dead,
    Tremendous still in death.

Ah, what was then Llewellyn's pain!
    For now the truth was clear;
His gallant hound the wolf had slain
    To save Llewellyn's heir.

William Robert Spencer wrote much deft, polished verse in his day. Indeed, Lord Byron termed Spencer "the perfect aristocrat," not only for his elevated verse, but also for his lofty status in British society.

The rhymed folk tale of "Beth-Gêlert" is the only poem of Spencer's which is still read. Its Saxon setting is no doubt a product of the same fashion for "life in Old England" that moved Scott to pen "Lochinvar." The name of Spencer's poem gave scholars a clue to the nature of the hero—in old Saxon, "Beth-Gêlert" means "brightest among the smartest."

The Cremation of Sam McGee

ROBERT SERVICE (1874-1958)

There are strange things done in the midnight sun
  By the men who moil for gold
The Arctic trails have their secret tales
  That would make your blood run cold
The Northern Lights have seen queer sights,
  But the queerest they ever did see
Was that night on the marge of Lake Lebarge
  I cremated Sam McGee.

Now Sam McGee was from Tennessee, where the
  cotton blooms and blows.
Why he left his home in the South to roam 'round the
  Pole, God only knows.
He was always cold, but the land of gold seemed to
  hold him like a spell;
Though he'd often say in his homely way that "he'd
  sooner live in hell."

On a Christmas Day we were mushing our way over
  the Dawson trail.
Talk of your cold! through the parka's fold it stabbed
  like a driven nail.

If our eyes we'd close, then the lashes froze till
    sometimes we couldn't see;
It wasn't much fun, but the only one to whimper was
    Sam McGee.

And that very night, as we lay packed tight in our
    robes beneath the snow,
And the dogs were fed, and the stars o'erhead were
    dancing heel and toe,
He turned to me, and "Cap," says he, "I'll cash in this
    trip, I guess;
And if I do, I'm asking that you won't refuse my last
    request."

Well, he seemed so low that I couldn't say no; then he
    says with a sort of moan:
"It's the cursed cold, and it's got right hold till I'm
    chilled clean through to the bone.
Yet 'tain't being dead—it's my awful dread of the icy
    grave that pains;
So I want you to swear that, foul or fair, you'll
    cremate my last remains."

A pal's last need is a thing to heed, so I swore I would
    not fail;
And we started on at the streak of dawn; but God! he
    looked ghastly pale.
He crouched on the sleigh, and he raved all day of his
    home in Tennessee;
And before nightfall a corpse was all that was left of
    Sam McGee.

There wasn't a breath in that land of death, and I
    hurried, horror-driven,
With a corpse half hid that I couldn't get rid, because
    of a promise given;
It was lashed to the sleigh, and it seemed to say: "You
    may tax your brawn and brains,
But you promised true, and it's up to you to cremate
    those last remains."

Now a promise made is a debt unpaid, and the trail
    has its own stern code.
In the days to come, though my lips were dumb, in
    my heart how I cursed that load.
In the long, long night, by the lone firelight, while the
    huskies, round in a ring,
Howled out their woes to the homeless snows—O
    God! how I loathed the thing.

And every day that quiet clay seemed to heavy and
    heavier grow;
And on I went, though the dogs were spent and the
    grub was getting low;
The trail was bad, and I felt half mad, but I swore I
    would not give in;
And I'd often sing to the hateful thing, and it
    harkened with a grin.

Till I came to the marge of Lake Lebarge, and a
    derelict there lay;
It was jammed in the ice, but I saw in a trice it was
    called the "Alice May."

And I looked at it, and I thought a bit, and I looked at
    my frozen chum;
Then "Here," said I, with a sudden cry, "is my cre-
    ma-tor-eum."

Some planks I tore from the cabin floor, and I lit the
    boiler fire;
Some coal I found that was lying around, and I
    heaped the fuel higher;
The flames just soared, and the furnace roared—such
    a blaze you seldom see;
And I burrowed a hole in the glowing coal, and I
    stuffed in Sam McGee.

Then I made a hike, for I didn't like to hear him sizzle
    so;
And the heavens scowled, and the huskies howled,
    and the wind began to blow.
It was icy cold, but the hot sweat rolled down my
    cheeks, and I don't know why;
And the greasy smoke in an inky cloak went streaking
    down the sky.

I do not know how long in the snow I wrestled with
    grisly fear;
But the stars came out and they danced about ere
    again I ventured near;
I was sick with dread, but I bravely said: "I'll just take
    a peep inside.
I guess he's cooked, and it's time I looked;" . . . then
    the door I opened wide.

And there sat Sam, looking cool and calm, in the
     heart of the furnace roar;
And he wore a smile you could see a mile, and he
     said: "Please close that door.
It's fine in here, but I greatly fear you'll let in the cold
     and storm!
Since I left Plumtree, down in Tennessee, it's the first
     time I've been warm."

There are strange things done in the midnight sun
     By the men who moil for gold;
The Arctic trails have their secret tales
     That would make your blood run cold;
The Northern Lights have seen queer sights,
     But the queerest they ever did see
Was that night on the marge of Lake Lebarge
     I cremated Sam McGee.

This grisly yarn first appeared in Songs of a Sourdough *(1907), reprinted eight years later as* The Spell of the Yukon. *The poem is notable for the way Service releases the macabre tension in the stanza before the refrain, and for the deft use of mid-line rhyme throughout the poem.*

The first poem of Songs of a Sourdough *supplies a vivid setting for Service's desolate Yukon ballads. Titled "The Land God Forgot," it concludes:*

> O outcast land! O leper land!
> Let the lone wolf-cry all express
> The hate insensate of thy hand,
> Thy heart's abysmal loneliness.

For a biographical note on Service, see page 28.

"Curfew Must Not Ring Tonight"

ROSE HARTWICK THORPE (1850-1939)

Slowly England's sun was setting o'er the hilltops far
away,
Filling all the land with beauty at the close of one sad
day;
And the last rays kissed the forehead of a man and a
maiden fair,
He with footsteps slow and weary, she with sunny
floating hair;
He with bowed head, sad and thoughtful, she with
lips all cold and white,
Struggling to keep back the murmur, "Curfew must
not ring tonight!"

"Sexton," Bessie's white lips faltered, pointing to the
prison old,
With its turrets tall and gloomy, with its walls, dark,
damp and cold—
"I've a lover in the prison, doomed this very night to
die
At the ringing of the curfew, and no earthly help is
nigh!
Cromwell will not come till sunset"; and her face
grew strangely white
As she breathed the husky whisper, "Curfew must
not ring tonight!"

"Bessie," calmly spoke the sexton—and his accents
    pierced her heart
Like the piercing of an arrow, like a deadly poisoned
    dart—
"Long, long years I've rung the curfew from that
    gloomy, shadowed tower;
Every evening, just at sunset, it has told the twilight
    hour;
I have done my duty ever, tried to do it just and
    right—
Now I'm old I still must do it: Curfew, girl, must ring
    tonight!"

Wild her eyes and pale her features, stern and white
    her thoughtful brow,
And within her secret bosom Bessie made a solemn
    vow.
She had listened while the judges read, without a tear
    or sigh,
"At the ringing of the curfew, Basil Underwood must
    die."
And her breath came fast and faster, and her eyes
    grew large and bright,
As in undertone she murmured, "Curfew must not
    ring tonight!"

With quick step she bounded forward, sprang within
    the old church door,
Left the old man threading slowly paths he'd often
    trod before;

Not one moment paused the maiden, but with eye
and cheek aglow
Mounted up the gloomy tower, where the bell swung
to and fro
As she climbed the dusty ladder, on which fell no ray
of light,
Up and up, her white lips saying, "Curfew shall not
ring tonight!"

She has reached the topmost ladder, o'er her hangs
the great dark bell:
Awful is the gloom beneath her, like the pathway
down to hell!
Lo, the ponderous tongue is swinging. 'Tis the hour
of curfew now,
And the sight has chilled her bosom, stopped her
breath and paled her brow;
Shall she let it ring? No, never! Flash her eyes with
sudden light,
And she springs and grasps it firmly: "Curfew shall
not ring tonight!"

Out she swung, far out; the city seemed a speck of
light below;
She 'twixt heaven and earth suspended as the bell
swung to and fro;
And the sexton at the bell rope, old and deaf, heard
not the bell,
But he thought it still was ringing fair young Basil's
funeral knell.

Still the maiden clung more firmly, and, with
    trembling lips and white,
Said, to hush her heart's wild beating, "Curfew shall
    not ring tonight!"

It was o'er; the bell ceased swaying, and the maiden
    stepped once more
Firmly on the dark old ladder, where for hundred
    years before
Human foot had not been planted; but the brave
    deed she had done
Should be told long ages after—often as the setting
    sun
Should illume the sky with beauty, aged sires, with
    heads of white,
Long should tell the little children, " Curfew did not
    ring that night."

O'er the distant hills came Cromwell; Bessie sees
    him, and her brow,
Full of hope and full of gladness, has no anxious
    traces now.
At his feet she tells her story, shows her hands all
    bruised and torn;
And her face so sweet and pleading, yet with sorrow
    pale and worn,
Touched his heart with sudden pity—lit his eye with
    misty light;
"Go, your lover lives!" said Cromwell; "Curfew shall
    not ring tonight!"

Rose Hartwick Thorpe wrote many poems and novels throughout her long career, but what measure of fame she retains is based solely on "Curfew Must Not Ring Tonight," which she wrote as an Indiana girl of seventeen. Her ballad of Protectorate England was published in a Detroit newspaper, and soon met with international acclaim.

Several variants appeared, credited to but seemingly not written by Mrs. Thorpe. One of these concludes:

> Wide they flung the massive portals, led the
>   prisoner forth to die,
> All his bright young life before him. 'Neath
>   the darkening English sky
> Bessie came with flying footsteps, eyes
>   aglow with love-light sweet;
> Kneeling on the turf beside him, laid a
>   pardon at his feet.
> In his brave, strong arms he clasped her,
>   kissed the face upturned and white,
> Whispered, "Darling, you have saved me;
>   curfew will not ring tonight."

The Goat and the Three Red Shirts

ANONYMOUS

There was a man, now please to note,
There was a man, who had a goat;
He loved that goat, indeed he did,
He loved that goat, just like a kid.

One day that goat felt frisk and fine,
Ate three red shirts from off the line.
The man he grabbed him by the back,
And tied him to a railroad track.

But when the train hove into sight,
That goat grew pale and green with fright.
He heaved a sign, as if in pain,
Coughed up those shirts and flagged the train!

This small tall tale is in the tradition of such whoppers as Paul Bunyan, *"The Notorious Jumping Frog of Calaveras County," and "Clementine." For a longer, more elaborate version of this story, see Robert Service's "Ballad of Casey's Billy Goat," in his* Bar-Room Ballads.

If—

RUDYARD KIPLING (1865-1936)

If you can keep your head when all about you
    Are losing theirs and blaming it on you;
If you can trust yourself when all men doubt you,
    But make allowance for their doubting too;
If you can wait and not be tired by waiting,
    Or, being lied about, don't deal in lies,
Or, being hated, don't give way to hating,
    And yet don't look too good, nor talk too wise;

If you can dream—and not make dreams your
master;
    If you can think—and not make thoughts your aim;
If you can meet with triumph and disaster
    And treat those two impostors just the same;
If you can bear to hear the truth you've spoken
    Twisted by knaves to make a trap for fools,
Or watch the things you gave your life to broken,
    And stoop and build 'em up with wornout tools;

If you can make one heap of all your winnings
    And risk it on one turn of pitch-and-toss,
And lose, and start again at your beginnings
    And never breathe a word about your loss;
If you can force your heart and nerve and sinew
    To serve your turn long after they are gone,

And so hold on when there is nothing in you
  Except the Will which says to them: "Hold on";

If you can talk with crowds and keep your virtue,
  Or walk with kings—nor lose the common touch;
If neither foes nor loving friends can hurt you;
  If all men count with you, but none too much;
If you can fill the unforgiving minute
  With sixty seconds' worth of distance run—
Yours is the Earth and everything that's·in it,
  And—which is more—you'll be a Man, my son!

*Rudyard Kipling was born in Bombay, went to England for his education, and returned to India in 1882, where he edited a paper in Lahore. His first poems and stories reflected the life of an Englishman in India—*Departmental Ditties, Barrack Room Ballads, Soldiers Three, *and others. Kipling's patriotic portraits of his fellow colonizers won him much popularity back in England, where he finally settled in 1900.*

"If" is undoubtedly one of the grandest inspirational poems ever written. It first appeared in book form in 1910, three years after Kipling became England's first winner of the Nobel Prize for Literature.

The Raven

EDGAR ALLAN POE (1809-1849)

Once upon a midnight dreary, while I pondered,
    weak and weary,
Over many a quaint and curious volume of forgotten
    lore,—
While I nodded, nearly napping, suddenly there
    came a tapping,
As of some one gently rapping, rapping at my
    chamber door.
"'Tis some visitor," I muttered, "tapping at my
    chamber door;
        Only this, and nothing more."

Ah, distinctly I remember, it was in the bleak
    December,
And each separate dying ember wrought its ghost
    upon the floor.
Eagerly I wished the morrow; vainly I had sought to
    borrow
From my books surcease of sorrow,—sorrow for the
    lost Lenore,—
For the rare and radiant maiden whom the angels
    named Lenore,—
        Nameless here forevermore.

And the silken, sad, uncertain rustling of each purple
 curtain
Thrilled me,—filled me with fantastic terrors never
 felt before;
So that now, to still the beating of my heart, I stood
 repeating,
"'Tis some visitor entreating entrance at my chamber
 door,—
Some late visitor entreating entrance at my chamber
 door;
   That it is, and nothing more."

Presently my soul grew stronger; hesitating then no
 longer,
"Sir," said I, "or madam, truly your forgiveness I
 implore;
But the fact is, I was napping, and so gently you came
 rapping,
And so faintly you came tapping, tapping at my
 chamber door,
That I scarce was sure I heard you."—Here I opened
 wide the door;
   Darkness there, and nothing more.

Deep into that darkness peering, long I stood there,
 wondering, fearing,
Doubting, dreaming dreams no mortal ever dared to
 dream before;

But the silence was unbroken, and the darkness gave
no token,
And the only word there spoken was the whispered
word "Lenore!"
This I whispered, and an echo murmured back the
word "Lenore!"
  Merely this, and nothing more.

Back into the chamber turning, all my soul within me
burning,
Soon again I heard a tapping, something louder than
before:
"Surely," said I, "surely that is something at my
window-lattice;
Let me see then what thereat is, and this mystery
explore,—
Let my heart be still a moment, and this mystery
explore;—
  'Tis the wind, and nothing more."

Open then I flung the shutter, when, with many a flirt
and flutter,
In there stepped a stately raven of the saintly days of
yore.
Not the least obeisance made he; not an instant
stopped or stayed he;
But, with mien of lord or lady, perched above my
chamber door,—
Perched upon a bust of Pallas, just above my
chamber door,—
  Perched, and sat, and nothing more.

Then this ebony bird
    beguiling my sad
    fancy into smil-
    ing,
By the grave and stern
    decorum of the
    countenance it wore,
"Though thy crest be shorn and shaven, thou," I said,
    "art sure no craven;
Ghastly, grim, and ancient raven, wandering from
    the nightly shore,
Tell me what thy lordly name is on the night's
    Plutonian shore?"
            Quoth the raven, "Nevermore!"

Much I marvelled this ungainly fowl to hear
    discourse so plainly,
Though its answer little meaning, little relevancy
    bore;

For we cannot help agreeing that no living human
    being
Ever yet was blessed with seeing bird above his
    chamber door,
Bird or beast upon the sculptured bust above his
    chamber door,
        With such name as "Nevermore!"

But the raven, sitting lonely on the placid bust, spoke
    only
That one word, as if his soul in that one word he did
    outpour.
Nothing further then he uttered,—not a feather then
    he fluttered,—
Till I scarcely more than muttered, "Other friends
    have flown before,—
On the morrow he will leave me, as my hopes have
    flown before."
        Then the bird said, "Nevermore!"

Startled at the stillness, broken by reply so aptly
    spoken,
"Doubtless," said I, "what it utters is its only stock
    and store,
Caught from some unhappy master, whom unmer-
    ciful disaster
Followed fast and followed faster, till his song one
    burden bore,
Till the dirges of his hope that melancholy burden
    bore,—
        Of "Nevermore,—nevermore!"

But the raven still beguiling all my sad soul into
    smiling,
Straight I wheeled a cushioned seat in front of bird
    and bust and door,
Then, upon the velvet sinking, I betook myself to
    linking
Fancy unto fancy, thinking what this ominous bird of
    yore—
What this grim, ungainly, ghastly, gaunt, and
    ominous bird of yore—
        Meant in croaking "Nevermore!"

This I sat engaged in guessing, but no syllable
    expressing
To the fowl whose fiery eyes now burned into my
    bosom's core;
This and more I sat divining, with my head at ease
    reclining
On the cushion's velvet lining that the lamplight
    gloated o'er,
But whose velvet violet lining, with the lamplight
    gloating o'er,
        She shall press—ah! nevermore!

Then methought the air grew denser, perfumed from
    an unseen censer,
Swung by seraphim, whose footfalls tinkled on the
    tufted floor.
"Wretch," I cried, "thy God hath lent thee,—by these
    angels he hath sent thee

Respite,—respite and nepenthe from the memories
　　of Lenore!
Quaff, O, quaff this kind nepenthe, and forget this
　　lost Lenore!"
　　　　　　Quoth the raven, "Nevermore!"

"Prophet!" said I, "thing of evil!—prophet still, if
　　bird or devil!
Whether tempter sent, or whether tempest tossed
　　thee here ashore,
Desolate yet all undaunted, on this desert land
　　enchanted,—
On this home by horror haunted,—tell me truly, I
　　implore,—
Is there—is there balm in Gilead?—tell me,—tell me,
　　I implore!"
　　　　　　Quoth the raven, "Nevermore!"

"Prophet!" said I, "thing of evil!—prophet still, if
　　bird or devil!
By that heaven that bends above us,—by that God
　　we both adore,
Tell this soul with sorrow laden, if, within the distant
　　Aidenn,
It shall clasp a sainted maiden, whom the angels
　　name Lenore,
Clasp a fair and radiant maiden, whom the angels
　　name Lenore!"
　　　　　　Quoth the raven, "Nevermore!"

"Be that word our sign of parting, bird or fiend!" I
    shrieked, upstarting,—
"Get thee back into the tempest and the night's
    Plutonian shore!
Leave no black plume as a token of that lie thy soul
    hath spoken!
Leave my loneliness unbroken!—quit the bust above
    my door!

Take thy beak from out my heart, and take thy form
    from off my door!"
            Quoth the raven, "Nevermore!"

And the raven, never flitting, still is sitting, still is
    sitting
On the pallid bust of Pallas, just above my chamber
    door;
And his eyes have all the seeming of a demon that is
    dreaming,
And the lamplight o'er him streaming throws his
    shadow on the floor;
And my soul from out that shadow that lies floating
    on the floor
            Shall be lifted—*nevermore!*

*Edgar Allan Poe has earned almost as much fame—
or notoriety—for his wayward life and pathetic
death as for his numerous works of genius. Orphaned
at two, he was brought up in Richmond, Virginia, by
his godfather John Allan and his wife. He entered the
University of Virginia in 1826, and one year later
published an anonymous book of verse,* Tamerlane
and Other Poems—*now perhaps the single most
valuable American volume to rare-book collectors.
After his expulsion from West Point in 1831, he went
to Baltimore, where he lived in a garret and began the
heavy drinking which was to prove his ruin.*

Poe's tragedy was that he could not "hold" even the smallest amount of liquor, yet he could not bring himself to quit drinking. At last, a ravaged man, he joined the Sons of Temperance, but the conversion didn't take. A last debauch in Baltimore—on his way north for his wedding—left him in a coma from which he did not emerge.

Poe served as an editor in Richmond, Philadelphia, and New York, gradually winning fame for such magazine stories as "The Murders in the Rue Morgue," "The Tell-Tale Heart," "The Gold Bug," and "The Pit and the Pendulum." The grotesquerie and terrible beauty of these stories also characterized his poems, notably "The Raven." Other poems for which Poe has been hailed—notably by the French— are "Annabel Lee," "To Helen," "The Bells," and "The City in the Sea."

Ozymandias

PERCY BYSSHE SHELLEY (1792-1822)

I met a traveler from an antique land,
Who said: Two vast and trunkless legs of stone
Stand in the desert. Near them, on the sand,
Half sunk, a shattered visage lies, whose frown,
And wrinkled lip, and sneer of cold command,
Tell that its sculptor well those passions read,
Which yet survive, stamped on these lifeless things,
The hand that mocked them, and the heart that fed:
And on the pedestal these words appear:
"My name is Ozymandias, King of Kings:
Look on my works, ye Mighty, and despair!"
Nothing beside remains. Round the decay
Of that colossal wreck, boundless and bare
The lone and level sands stretch far away.

Percy Bysshe Shelley was a precocious and sensitive child who could not endure the cruelties of the traditional "fagging" system at Eton, and in response developed a fierce resistance to arbitrary authority. In 1811, he wrote a pamphlet entitled "The Necessity of Atheism" which resulted in his expulsion from Oxford. That same year, he married the sixteen-year-old Harriet Westbrook to rescue her from the tyranny of her father.

Shelley's passionate nature ruled his life as well as his verse. In 1814, he abandoned his wife to run off with Mary Wollstonecraft Godwin, the daughter of the revolutionist William Godwin. Two years later, Harriet was discovered drowned in the Serpentine River. Fanny Godwin, sister of Mary, also killed herself in that year, probably for love of Shelley.

Denied custody of the two children Harriet bore him, Shelley exiled himself and Mary to Italy in 1818. Like his friend Byron, he was never to return to England. On July 1, 1822, Shelley and Edward Williams sailed across the Bay of Spezzia to greet Byron and Leigh Hunt, just arrived at Leghorn. On July 8, Shelley and Williams started to return, but they were never again seen alive. Their boat the Ariel sank, and the two bodies washed ashore weeks later.

In addition to "Ozymandias," a fine comment on the evanescence of fame and power, Shelley is know for his dramas Prometheus Unbound, The Cenci, *and* Hellas, *and for his poems "To a Skylark," "To Night," "Ode to the West Wind," and "Music, When Soft Voices Die."*

The Ballad of Charity

CHARLES GODFREY LELAND (1824-1903)

It was in a pleasant depot, sequestered from the rain,
That many weary passengers were waiting for the
    train;
Piles of quite expensive baggage, many a gorgeous
    portmanteau,
Ivory-handled umberellas made a most touristic
    show.

Whereunto there came a person, very humble was his
    mien,
Who took an observation of the interesting scene;
Closely scanned the umberellas, watched with joy
    the mighty trunks,
And observed that all the people were securing
    Pullman bunks.

Who was followed shortly after by a most unhappy
    tramp,
Upon whose features Poverty had jounced her iron
    stamp;
And to make a clear impression as bees sting while
    they buzz,
She had hit him rather harder than she generally
    does.

For he was so awfully ragged, and in parts so awfully
    bare,
That the folks were quite repulsioned to behold him
    begging there;
And instead of drawing currency from out of their
    pocket-books,
They drew themselves asunder with aversionary
    looks.

Sternly gazed the first newcomer on the unindulgent
    crowd,
Then in tones which pierced the depot he sililicussed
    aloud:—
"I have traveled o'er this continent from Quebec to
    Saginaw,
But such a set of scalawags as these I never saw!

"You are wealthy, you are loaded, you have houses,
    lands and rent,
Yet unto a suffering mortal, you will not donate a
    cent;

You expend your missionaries all the way to Tim-
buktu,
But there isn't any heathen that is half as small as you.

"You are lucky—you have check-books and deposits
in the bank,
And ye squanderate your money like titled folks of
rank;
The onyx and the sardonyx upon your garments
shine,
And you drink cocktails at dinner and wash them
down with wine.

"You are going for the summer to the islands by the
sea,
Where a sandwich sells for two bucks, and it's fifty
cents for tea;
Ivory-handled umberellas do not come into my plan,
But I can give some comfort to my suffering fellow
man.

"Handbags made of alligator are not truly at my call,
Yet in the eyes of Mercy, I am richer than you all,
For I can give five dollars where you cannot stand a
dime,
And never miss it neither, nor regret it any time."

Saying this he drew a wallet from inside his fancy
vest,
And gave the tramp a V-note which it was his level
best;

Other people having seen him, soon to charity
inclined—
One genuine real giver makes a hundred change their
mind.

The first who gave five dollars led the other one
about,
And at every contribution, he a-raised a joyful shout;
Exclaiming how 'twas noble to relieviate distress,
And remarking that our duty is our present hap-
piness.

Eight hundred bucks in greenbacks were collected
by the tramp,
When he bid them all good evening, and went out
into the damp;
And was followed briefly after by the one who made
the speech,
And who showed by good example how to practise
as to preach.

Which soon around the corner the couple quickly
met,
And the tramp produced the specie for to liquidate
his debt;
And the man who did the preaching took five
hundred of the sum,
Which five from eight collected left three hundred
for the bum.

And the couple passed the summer at the seashore
    with the rest;
Greatly changed in their appearance and most
    elegantly dressed.
Any fowl with change of feathers may a brilliant bird
    become:
Oh, how hard is life for many! Oh, how sweet it is for
    some!

Charles Godfrey Leland is perhaps best known for his "Hans Breitmann Ballads," humorous poems in Germanic pidgin English. However, Leland was an accomplished translator and produced more than 50 books, most of them on language and folklore. Moreover, he was a passionate abolitionist who founded the Continental Magazine *in 1862 to further the Union cause.*

For all his serious pursuits, Leland's most lasting work is humorous. "The Ballad of Charity" is a fine example of his sardonic view of the struggle for the almighty dollar.

The Hell-Gate of Soissons

HERBERT KAUFMAN (1878-1947)

My name is Darino, the poet. You have heard? *Oui,
Comédie Française.*
Perchance it has happened, *mon ami,* you know of
my unworthy lays.
Ah, then you must guess how my fingers are itching
to talk to a pen;
For I was at Soissons, and saw it, the death of the
twelve Englishmen.

My leg, *malheureusement,* I left it behind on the
banks of the Aisne.
Regret? I would pay with the other to witness their
valor again.
A trifle, indeed, I assure you, to give for the honor to
tell
How that handful of British, undaunted, went into
the Gateway of Hell.

Let me draw you a plan of the battle. Here we French
and your Engineers stood;
Over there a detachment of German sharpshooters
lay hid in a wood.
A *mitrailleuse* battery planted on top of this well-
chosen ridge
Held the road for the Prussians and covered the
direct approach to the bridge.

103

It was madness to dare the dense murder that
    spewed from those ghastly machines.
(Only those who have danced to its music can know
    what the *mitrailleuse* means.)
But the bridge on the Aisne was a menace; our safety
    demanded its fall:
"Engineers—volunteers!" In a body, the Royals
    stood out at the call.

Death at best was the fate of that mission—to their
    glory not one was dismayed.
A party was chosen—and seven survived till the
    powder was laid.
And *they* died with their fuses unlighted. Another
    detachment! Again
A sortie is made—all too vainly. The bridge still
    commanded the Aisne.

We were fighting two foes—Time and Prussia—the
    moments were worth more than troops.
We *must* blow up the bridge. A lone soldier darts out
    from the Royals and swoops
For the fuse! Fate seems with us. We cheer him; he
    answers—our hopes are reborn!
A ball rips his visor—his khaki shows red where
    another has torn.

Will he live—will he last—will he make it? *Hélas!*
    And so near to the goal!
A second, he dies! then a third one! A fourth! Still the
    Germans take toll!

A fifth, *magnifique!* It is magic! How does he escape
    them? He may . . .
Yes, he *does!* See, the match flares! A rifle rings out
    from the wood and says "Nay!"

Six, seven, eight, nine take their places; six, seven,
    eight, nine brave their hail:
Six, seven, eight, nine—how we count them! But the
    sixth, seventh, eighth, and ninth fail!
A tenth! *Sacré nom!* But these English are soldiers—
    they know how to try;
(He fumbles the place where his jaw was)—they
    show, too, how heroes can die.

Ten we count—ten who ventured unquailing—ten
    there were—and ten are no more!
Yet another salutes and superbly essays where the ten
    failed before.
God of Battles, look down and protect him! Lord, his
    heart is as Thine—let him live!
But the *mitrailleuse* splutters and stutters, and riddles
    him into a sieve.

Then I thought of my sins, and sat waiting the charge
    that we could not withstand.
And I thought of my beautiful Paris, and gave a last
    look at the land,
At France, my *belle France,* in her glory of blue sky
    and green field and wood.
Death with honor, but never surrender. And to die
    with such men—it was good.

They are forming—the bugles are blaring—they will
　　cross in a moment and then—
When out of the line of the Royals (your island, *mon
　　ami,* breeds men)
Bursts a private, a tawny-haired giant—it was
　　hopeless, but *ciel?* how he ran!
Bon Dieu please remember the pattern, and make
　　many more on his plan!

No cheers from our ranks, and the Germans, they
　　halted in wonderment, too;
See, he reaches the bridge; ah! he lights it! I am
　　dreaming, it *cannot* be true.
Screams of rage! *Fusillade!* They have killed him!
　　Too late though, the good work is done.
By the valor of twelve English martyrs, the Hell-Gate
　　of Soissons is won!

Herbert Kaufman was an American journalist who specialized in international reporting. When World War I broke out, he sent back his war reports to the U. S. for syndication. It was during this time that "Hell-Gate of Soissons" made its initial appearance in Britain, under the title "Song of the Guns." It soon became popular on both sides of the Atlantic, particularly as a recitation. In fact, the drama and pathos of the poem cannot be appreciated through a silent reading, in which Kaufman's highly charged verse merely seems metrically flawed.

Soissons is a smallish city in the north of France, on the Aisne River. The stormy history of this old Roman town is marked by several sieges and changes of rulers.

The Enchanted Shirt

JOHN HAY (1838-1905)

The King was sick. His cheek was red
  And his eye was clear and bright;
He ate and drank with a kingly zest,
  And peacefully snored at night.

But he said he was sick, and a king should know,
  And doctors came by the score.
They did not cure him. He cut off their heads
  And sent to the schools for more.

At last two famous doctors came,
  And one was as poor as a rat,—
He had passed his life in studious toil,
  And never found time to grow fat.

The other had never looked in a book;
  His patients gave him no trouble,—
If they recovered they paid him well,
  If they died their heirs paid double.

Together they looked at the royal tongue,
  As the King on his couch reclined;
In succession they thumped his august chest,
  But no trace of disease could find.

The old sage said, "You're as sound as a nut."
  "Hang him up," roared the King in a gale,—
In a ten-knot gale of royal rage;
  The other leech grew a shade pale,

But he pensively rubbed his sagacious nose,
  And thus his prescription ran,—
The King will be well, if he sleeps one night
  In the Shirt of a Happy Man.

Wide o'er the realm the couriers rode,
  And fast their horses ran,
And many they saw, and to many they spoke,
  But they found no Happy Man.

They found poor men who would fain be rich,
  And rich who thought they were poor;
And men who twisted their waists in stays,
  And women that shortthose wore.

They saw two men by the roadside sit,
  And both bemoaned their lot;
For one had buried his wife, he said,
  And the other one had not.

At last as they came to a village gate,—
  A beggar lay whistling there;
He whistled and sang and laughed and rolleded
  On the grass in the soft June air.

The weary couriers paused and looked
  At the scamp so blithe and gay;
And one of them said, "Heaven save you, friend!
  You seem to be happy to-day."

"O yes, fair sirs," the rascal laughed
  And his voice rang free and glad;
"An idle man has so much to do
  That he never has time to be sad."

"This is our man," the courier said;
  "Our luck has led us aright.
"I will give you a hundred ducats, friend,
  For the loan of your shirt to-night."

The merry blackguard lay back on the grass,
  And laughed till his face was black;
"I would do it, God wot," and he roared with the fun,
  "But I haven't a shirt to my back."

Each day to the King the reports came in
  Of his unsuccessful spies,
And the sad panorama of human woes
  Passed daily under his eyes.

And he grew ashamed of his useless life,
  And his maladies hatched in gloom;
He opened his windows and let the air
  Of the free heaven into his room.

And out he went in the world and toiled
   In his own appointed way;
And the people blessed him, the land was glad,
   And the King was well and gay.

John Hay was one of America's most remarkable men. He served as a private secretary to Lincoln between 1861 and 1865, an experience which— twenty-five years later—led to his monumental ten-volume biography of the President, written with John G. Nicolay. He wrote for the New York Tribune *for four years, and published a significant book on Spain,* Castilian Days. *Moreover, Hay was Assistant Secretary of State to President Hayes, ambassador to Great Britain under McKinley, and from 1898 to 1905, Secretary of State to McKinley and then Theodore Roosevelt. In the diplomatic realm, he is best known for his formulation of the "Open-Door Policy" toward China.*

As a poet and humorist, Hay is remembered not only for the verse fable above, but also for his Pike County Ballads *of 1871, among them "Little Breeches" and "Jim Bludso of the Prairie Belle."*

The Society
upon the Stanislaus

BRET HARTE (1836-1902)

I reside at Table Moutain, and my name is Truthful
    James;
I am not up to small deceit, or any sinful games;
And I'll tell in simple language what I know about the
    row
That broke up our society upon the Stanislow.

But first I would remark that it is not a proper plan
For any scientific gent to whale his fellow man,
And if a member don't agree with his peculiar whim,
To lay for that same member, so to razzle-dazzle
    him.

Now, nothing could be finer or more beautiful to see
Than the first six months' proceedings of that same
    society;
Till Brown of Calaveras brought a lot of fossil bones
That he found within a tunnel near the residence of
    Jones.

Then Brown he read a paper, and he reconstructed
    there,
From those same bones, an animal that was
    extremely rare;
And Jones then asked the Chair for a suspension of
    the rules,
Till he could prove that those same bones was one of
    his lost mules.

Then Brown, he smiled a bitter smile, and said he was
    at fault,
It seemed he had been trespassing on Jones's family
    vault;
He was a most sarcastic man, this quiet Mr. Brown;
He had the kind of acrid smile that almost was a
    frown.

Now, I hold it is not decent for a scientific gent
To say another is an ass—at least, to all intent;
Nor should the individual who happens to be meant
Reply by heaving rocks at him to any great extent.

Then Abner Deal of Angel's raised a point of order,
      when
A chunk of old red sandstone took him in the
      abdomen;
And he smiled a kind of sickly smile, and curled up
      on the floor,
And the subsequent proceedings interested him no
      more.

For in less time than I write it, every member did
      engage
In a warfare with the remnants of a palaeozoic age;
And the way they heaved those fossils in their anger
      was a sin,
Till the skull of an old mammoth caved the head of
      Thompson in.

And this is all I have to say of these improper games
For I live at Table Mountain, and my name is
    Truthful James;
And I've told, in simple language, what I know about
    the row
That broke up our society upon the Stanislow.

Francis Bret Harte, though regarded as a writer of the West, spent most of his life in the East and in Europe. His working days began at the age of 13, when he was a clerk in a lawyer's office in Albany, New York. Six more years of clerking and similarly tame labor convinced him to go West, where he worked as a miner, a printer, a teacher, and a journalist.

In 1868, he founded the Overland Monthly, *in which most of his famous stories and humorous verse appeared. Among his finest stories are "The Outcasts of Poker Flat" and "The Luck of Roaring Camp"; his poems include the tragic "Guild's Signal" and the slyly humorous "Plain Language from Truthful James."*

The Pied Piper of Hamelin

ROBERT BROWNING (1812-1889)

Hamelin Town's in Brunswick,
By famous Hanover city;
The river Weser, deep and wide,
Washes its wall on the southern side;
A pleasanter spot you never spied;
But, when begins my ditty,
Almost five hundred years ago,
To see the townsfolk suffer so
From vermin was a pity.

Rats!
They fought the dogs, and kill'd the cats,
And bit the babies in the cradles,
And ate the cheeses out of the vats,
And lick'd the soup from the cook's own ladles,
Split open the kegs of salted sprats,
Made nests inside men's Sunday hats,
And even spoil'd the women's chats,
By drowning their speaking
With shrieking and squeaking
In fifty different sharps and flats.

At last the people in a body
To the Town Hall came flocking:
" 'Tis clear," cried they, "our Mayor's a noddy;

　　And as for our Corporation—shocking
To think we buy gowns lined with ermine
For dolts that can't or won't determine
What's best to rid us of our vermin!
You hope, because you're old and obese,
To find in the furry civic robe ease?
Rouse up, sirs! Give your brains a racking
To find the remedy we're lacking,
Or, sure as fate, we'll send you packing!"
At this the Mayor and Corporation
Quaked with a mighty consternation.

An hour they sat in counsel,
　　At length the Mayor broke silence:
"For a guilder I'd my ermine gown sell;
　　I wish I were a mile hence!
It's easy to bid one rack one's brain—
I'm sure my poor head aches again,
I've scratch'd it so, and all in vain.
Oh for a trap, a trap, a trap!"
Just as he said this, what should hap
At the chamber-door but a gentle tap?
"Bless us!" cried the Mayor, "What's that?"
(With the Corporation as he sat,
Looking little though wondrous fat;
Nor brighter was his eye, nor moister
Than a too long-open'd oyster,
Save when at noon his paunch grew mutinous
For a plate of turtle, green and glutinous)
"Only a scraping of shoes on the mat?

Anything like the sound of a rat
Makes my heart go pit-a-pat!"
"Come in!"—the Mayor cried, looking bigger;
And in did come the strangest figure!
His queer long coat from heel to head
Was half of yellow and half of red;
And he himself was tall and thin,
With sharp blue eyes, each like a pin,
And light loose hair, yet swarthy skin,
No tuft on cheek nor beard on chin,
But lips where smiles went out and in—
There was no guessing his kith and kin!
And nobody could enough admire
The tall man and his quaint attire.
Quoth one: "It's as if my great-grandsire,
Starting up at the Trump of Doom's tone,
Had walk'd this way from his painted tombstone!"

He advanced to the council-table:
And, "Please your honors," said he, "I'm able,
By means of a secret charm, to draw
All creatures living beneath the sun,
That creep, or swim, or fly, or run,
After me so as you never saw!
And I chiefly use my charm
On creatures that do people harm,
The mole, and toad, and newt, and viper;
And people call me the Pied Piper."
(And here they noticed round his neck
A scarf of red and yellow stripe,
To match with his coat of the self-same check;

And at the scarf's end hung a pipe;
And his fingers, they noticed, were ever straying
As if impatient to be playing
Upon this pipe, as low it dangled
Over his vesture so old-fangled.)
"Yet," said he, "poor piper as I am,
In Tartary I freed the Cham,
Last June, from his huge swarm of gnats;
I eased in Asis the Nizam
Of a monstrous brook of vampire-bats;
And, as for what your brain bewilders—
If I can rid your town of rats,
Will you give me a thousand guilders?"
"One? fifty thousand!" was the exclamation
Of the astonished Mayor and Corporation.

Into the street the Piper stept,
　　Smiling first a little smile,
As if he knew what magic slept
　　In his quiet pipe the while;
Then, like a musical adept,
To blow the pipe his lips he wrinkled,
And green and blue his sharp eyes twinkled,
Like a candle-flame where salt is sprinkled;
And ere three shrill notes the pipe had utter'd,
You heard as if an army mutter'd;
And the muttering grew to a grumbling;
And the grumbling grew to a mighty rumbling;
And out of the houses the rats came tumbling.
Great rats, small rats, lean rats, brawny rats,

Brown rats, black rats, gray rats, tawny rats,
Grave old plodders, gay young friskers,
    Fathers, mothers, uncles, cousins,
Cocking tails and prickling whiskers,
    Families by tens and dozens,
Brothers, sisters, husbands, wives—
Follow'd the Piper for their lives.
From street to street he piped advancing,
And step for step they follow'd dancing,
Until they came to the river Weser,
Wherein all plunged and perish'd!
—Save one who, stout as Julius Caesar,
Swam across and lived to carry
(As the manuscript he cherish'd)
To Rat-land home his commentary,
Which was, "At the first shrill notes of the pipe,
I heard a sound as of scraping tripe,
And putting apples, wondrous ripe,
Into a cider press's gripe:
And a moving away of pickle-tub boards,
And a leaving ajar of conserve-cupboards,
And a drawing the corks of train-oil flasks,
And a breaking the hoops of butter-casks;
And it seemed as if a voice
(Sweeter far than by harp or by psaltery
Is breathed) call'd out, O rats, rejoice!
The world is grown to one vast dry-saltery!
So munch on, crunch on, take your nuncheon,
Breakfast, supper, dinner, luncheon!
And just as a bulky sugar-puncheon,
All ready staved, like a great sun shone

Glorious scarce an inch before me,
Just as methought it said, Come, bore me!
—I found the Weser rolling o'er me."

You should have heard the Hamelin people
Ringing the bells till they rock'd the steeple;
"Go," cried the Mayor, "and get long poles!
Consult with carpenters and builders,
And leave in our town not even a trace
Of the rats!"—when suddenly up the face
Of the Piper perk'd in the market-place,
With a, "First, if you please, my thousand guilders!"

A thousand guilders! The Mayor look'd blue;
So did the Corporation too.
For council dinners made rare havoc
With Claret, Moselle, Vin-de-Grave, Hock;
And half the money would replenish
Their cellar's biggest butt with Rhenish.
To pay this sum to a wandering fellow
With a gypsy coat of red and yellow!
"Beside," quoth the Mayor, with a knowing wink,
"Our business was done at the river's brink;
We saw with our eyes the vermin sink,
And what's dead can't come to life, I think.
So, friend, we're not the folks to shrink
From the duty of giving you something for drink,
And a matter of money to put in your poke;
But, as for the guilders, what we spoke
Of them, as you very well know, was in joke.
Beside, our losses have made us thrifty;
A thousand guilders! Come, take fifty!"

The Piper's face fell, and he cried,
"No trifling! I can't wait, beside!
I've promised to visit by dinnertime
Bagdad, and accept the prime
Of the Head Cook's pottage, all he's rich in,
For having left, in the Caliph's kitchen,
Of a nest of scorpions no survivor—
With him I proved no bargain-driver.
With you, don't think I'll bate a stiver!
And folks who put me in a passion
May find me pipe after another fashion."

"How?" cried the Mayor, "d'ye think I'll brook
Being worse treated than a Cook?
Insulted by a lazy ribald
With idle pipe and vesture piebald?
You threaten us, fellow? Do your worst,
Blow your pipe there till you burst!"

Once more he stept into the street;
    And to his lips again
    Laid his long pipe of smooth straight cane;
And ere he blew three notes (such sweet
Soft notes as yet musician's cunning
    Never gave the enraptured air)
There was a rustling, that seem'd like a bustling
Of merry crowds justling at pitching and hustling,
Small feet were pattering, wooden shoes clattering,
Little hands clapping, and little tongues chattering,
And like fowls in a farm-yard when barley is scat-
        tering,

Out came the children running.
All the little boys and girls,
With rosy cheeks and flaxen curls,
And sparkling eyes and teeth like pearls,
Tripping and skipping, ran merrily after
The wonderful music with shouting and laughter.

The Mayor was dumb, and the Council stood
As if they were changed into blocks of wood,   ·
Unable to move a step, or cry
To the children merrily skipping by
—Could only follow with the eye
That joyous crowd at the Piper's back.
But how the Mayor was on the rack,
And the wretched Council's bosoms beat,
As the Piper turn'd from the High Street
To where the Weser roll'd its waters
Right in the way of their sons and daughters!
However, he turned from south to west,
And to Koppelberg Hill his steps address'd,
And after him the children press'd;
Great was the joy in every breast.
"He never can cross that mighty top!
He's forced to let the piping drop,
And we shall see our children stop!"
When, lo, as they reach'd the mountain side,
A wondrous portal open'd wide,
As if a cavern was suddenly hollow'd;
And the Piper advanced and the children follow'd,
And when all were in to the very last,
The door in the mountain-side shut fast.

Did I say all? No! one was lame,
And could not dance the whole of the way,
And in after years, if you would blame
His sadness, he was used to say,
"It's dull in our town since my playmates left!
I can't forget that I'm bereft
Of all the pleasant sights they see,
Which the Piper also promised me,
For he led us, he said, to a joyous land,
Joining the town and just at hand,
Where waters gush'd and fruit trees grew,
And flowers put forth a fairer hue,
And everything was strange and new;
The sparrows were brighter than peacocks here,
And the dogs outran our fallow deer,
And honey-bees had lost their stings,
And horses were born with eagles' wings;

And just as I became assured
My lame foot would be speedily cured,
The music stopp'd, and I stood still,
And found myself outside the Hill,
Left alone against my will,
To go now limping as before,
And never hear of that country more!"

Alas, alas for Hamelin!
   There came into many a burgher's pate
   A text which says that Heaven's Gate
   Opes to the rich at as easy rate
As the needle's eye takes a camel in!
The Mayor sent east, west, north, and south
To offer the Piper by word of mouth,
   Wherever it was men's lot to find him,
Silver and gold to his heart's content,
If he'd only return the way he went,
   And bring the children behind him.
But when they saw 'twas a lost endeavor,
And Piper and dancers were gone forever,
They made a decree that lawyers never
   Should think their records dated duly
If, after the day of the month and year,
These words did not as well appear:
"And so long after what happen'd here
   On the twenty-second of July,
Thirteen hundred and Seventy-six":
And the better in memory to fix
The place of the children's last retreat,

They call'd it the Pied Piper's Street,
Where any one playing on pipe or tabor
Was sure for the future to lose his labor.
Nor suffer'd they hostelry or tavern
　To shock with mirth a street so solemn,
But opposite the place of the cavern
　They wrote the story on a column,
And on the great church-window painted
The same, to make the world acquainted
How their children were stolen away,
And there it stands to this very day.
And I must not omit to say
That in Transylvania there's a tribe
Of alien people that ascribe
The outlandish ways and dress
On which their neighbors lay such stress,
To their fathers and mothers having risen
Out of some subterranean prison,
Into which they were trepann'd
Long time ago in a mighty band
Out of Hamelin town in Brunswick land,
But how or why, they don't understand.

So, Willy, let me and you be wipers
Of scores out with all men—especially pipers!
And, whether they pipe us free, from rats or from
　　mice,
If we've promised them aught, let us keep our
　　promise.

Robert Browning's early verse was imitative of his boyhood idols, Byron and Shelley. But at the age of 23, he found his own style—dramatic, psychological, often abstruse—with the publication of Paracelsus. *In 1840, after two years in Italy, he published a poem of genius entitled* Sordello; *however, its involved rhythms and difficult phrasing gave Browning a reputation for obscurity which for twenty years he was unable to shake.*

At the time Browning eloped to Italy with Elizabeth Barrett in 1846, her reputation as a poet far exceeded his. This state prevailed throughout and even after their fifteen-year marriage (she died in 1861). It was not until the appearance of The Ring and the Book *in 1869 that Robert Browning's star began to rise among the general public, despite the fact that much of his best work had been written earlier. In his later years, Browning endured the adulation of a myriad of "Browning Clubs" in England and America.*

"The Pied Piper of Hamelin" is based on an old legend familiar to many cultures—the revenge of the magician who is cheated out of his promised reward. Browning wrote the poem for Willy—named in the last stanza—the son of the actor William Macready. Young Willy was ill, and had requested a subject for which he could draw pictures.

O Captain! My Captain!

WALT WHITMAN (1819-1892)

O Captain! my Captain! our fearful trip is done;
The ship has weather'd every rack, the prize we
    sought is won;
The port is near, the bells I hear, the people all
    exulting,
While follow eyes the steady keel, the vessel grim
    and daring:

      But O heart! heart! heart!
        O the bleeding drops of red,
          Where on the deck my Captain lies,
          Fallen cold and dead.

O Captain! my Captain! rise up and hear the bells;
Rise up—for you the flag is flung—for you the bugle
    trills;
For you bouquets and ribbon'd wreaths—for you the
    shores a-crowding;
For you they call, the swaying mass, their eager faces
    turning:

      Here Captain! dear father!
        This arm beneath your head;
          It is some dream that on the deck
          You've fallen cold and dead.

My captain does not answer, his lips are pale and still;
My father does not feel my arm, he has no pulse or
    will;
The ship is anchor'd safe and sound, its voyage
    closed and done;
From fearful trip the victor ship comes in with object
    won:

    Exult, O shores, and ring, O bells!
        But I, with mournful tread,
            Walk the deck my Captain lies,
                Fallen cold and dead.

Walt Whitman, America's "Good Gray Poet," was born on Long Island, but his family soon moved to Brooklyn. There he learned to set type, and at the age of fourteen he was employed in the composing room of the Long Island Star. *In the fifteen-odd years that followed, Whitman wrote baseball reports for the Brooklyn* Eagle, *temperance tracts for hire, and miscellaneous verse for his own pleasure. It was not until 1851, after a stint as reporter for the New Orleans* Crescent, *that Whitman threw over the white-collar life of the journalist for that of the common workman. In 1855, he published twelve poems in a volume called* Leaves of Grass. *Over the next thirty-seven years, this classic expanded to incorporate nearly 300 poems.*

"O Captain! My Captain!" is one of four MEMORIES OF PRESIDENT LINCOLN *included in the* DRUM TAPS *section of the fourth edition of* Leaves of Grass. *Another of the* MEMORIES *is "When Lilacs Last in the Dooryard Bloom'd," perhaps the greatest American elegy.*

Fleurette

ROBERT SERVICE (1874-1958)

My leg? It's off at the knee.
Do I miss it? Well, some. You see
I've had it since I was born;
And lately a devilish corn.
(I rather chuckle with glee
To think how I've fooled that corn.)

But I'll hobble around all right.
It isn't that, it's my face.
Oh I know I'm a hideous sight,
Hardly a thing in place;
Sort of gargoyle, you'd say.
Nurse won't give me a glass,
But I see the folks as they pass
Shudder and turn away;
Turn away in distress . . .
Mirror enough, I guess.

I'm gay! You bet I *am* gay;
But I wasn't a while ago.
If you'd seen me even to-day,
The darndest picture of woe,
With this Caliban mug of mine,
So ravaged and raw and red,
Turned to the wall—in fine,
Wishing that I was dead. . . .

What has happened since then,
Since I lay with my face to the wall,
The most despairing of men?
Listen! I'll tell you all.

That *poilu* across the way,
With the shrapnel wound in his head,
Has a sister: she came to-day
To sit awhile by his bed.
All morning I heard him fret:
"Oh, when will she come, Fleurette?"

Then sudden, a joyous cry;
The tripping of little feet;
The softest, tenderest sigh;
A voice so fresh and sweet;
Clear as a silver bell,
Fresh as the morning dews:
"C'est toi, c'est toi, Marcel!
Mon frère, comme je suis heureuse!"

So over the blanket's rim
I raised my terrible face,
And I saw—how I envied him!
A girl of such delicate grace;
Sixteen, all laughter and love;
As gay as a linnet, and yet
As tenderly sweet as a dove;
Half woman, half child—Fleurette.

Then I turned to the wall again.
(I was awfully blue, you see,)
And I thought with a bitter pain:
"Such visions are not for me."

So there like a log I lay,
All hidden, I thought, from view,
When sudden I heard her say:
"Ah! Who is that *malheureux?*"
Then briefly I heard him tell
(However he came to know)
How I'd smothered a bomb that fell
Into the trench, and so
None of my men were hit,
Though it busted me up a bit.

Well, I didn't quiver an eye,
And he chattered and there she sat;
And I fancied I heard her sigh—
But I wouldn't just swear to that.
And maybe she wasn't so bright,
Though she talked in a merry strain,
And I closed my eyes ever so tight,
Yet I saw her ever so plain:
Her dear little tilted nose,
Her delicate, dimpled chin,
Her mouth like a budding rose,
And the glistening pearls within;
Her eyes like the violet:
Such a rare little queen—Fleurette.

And at last when she rose to go,
The light was a little dim,
And I ventured to peep, and so
I saw her, graceful and slim,
And she kissed him and kissed him, and oh
How I envied and envied him!

So when she was gone I said
In rather a dreary voice
To him of the opposite bed:
"Ah, friend, how you must rejoice!
But me, I'm a thing of dread.
For me nevermore the bliss,
The thrill of a woman's kiss."

Then I stopped, for lo! she was there,
And a great light shone in her eyes.
And me! I could only stare,
I was taken so by surprise,
When gently she bent her head:
"May I kiss you, Sergeant?" she said.

Then she kissed my burning lips
With her mouth like a scented flower,
And I thrilled to the finger-tips,
And I hadn't even the power
To say: "God bless you, dear!"
And I felt such a precious tear
Fall on my withered cheek,
And darn it! I couldn't speak.

And so she went sadly away,
And I knew that my eyes were wet.
Ah, not to my dying day
Will I forget, forget!
Can you wonder now I am gay?
God bless her, that little Fleurette!

Service's experiences in the Ambulance Corps during World War I led to his Rhymes of a Red Cross Man, *of which "Fleurette" is one. Alternatingly coy, sentimental, gruesome, and heroic, "Fleurette" is a poem of contestable literary merit—as are many of* the poems in GREAT RECITATIONS—*but it is an undeniably powerful evocation of the horrors of war.*

In the verse foreword to Rhymes of a Red Cross Man, *Service says it best:*

And you yourself would mutter when
You took the things that once were men
And sped them through that zone of hate
To where the dripping surgeons wait;
And wonder too if in God's sight
War ever, ever can be right.

For a biographical note on Service, see page 28.

Boots

RUDYARD KIPLING (1865-1936)

We're foot—slog—slog—slog—sloggin' over Africa!
Foot—foot—foot—foot—sloggin' over Africa—
(Boots—boots—boots—boots, movin' up an' down
    again!)
       There's no discharge in the war!

Seven—six—eleven—five—nine-an'-twenty mile to-
    day—
Four—eleven—seventeen—thirty-two the day be-
    fore—
(Boots—boots—boots—boots, movin' up an' down
    again!)
       There's no discharge in the war!

Don't—don't—don't—don't—look at what's in front
    of you
(Boots—boots—boots—boots, movin' up an' down
    again);
Men—men—men—men—men go mad with watch-
    in' 'em,
       An' there's no discharge in the war!

Try—try—try—try—to think o' something dif-
    ferent—
Oh—my—God—keep—me from goin' lunatic!

(Boots—boots—boots—boots, movin' up an' down
   again!)
      There's no discharge in the war!

Count—count—count—count—the bullets in the
   bandoliers;
If—your—eyes—drop—they will get atop o' you
(Boots—boots—boots—boots, movin' up an' down
   again)—
      There's no discharge in the war!

We—can—stick—out—'unger, thirst, an' weariness,
But—not—not—not—not the chronic sight of 'em—
Boots—boots—boots—boots, movin' up an' down
   again,
      An' there's no discharge in the war!

'Tain't—so—bad—by—day because o' company,
But night—brings—long—strings o' forty thousand
   million
Boots—boots—boots—boots, movin' up an' down
   again.
      There's no discharge in the war!

I—'ave—marched—six—weeks in 'Ell an' certify
It—is—not—fire—devils, dark or anything
But boots—boots—boots, movin' up an' down again,
      An' there's no discharge in the war!

The boots that give this poem its march rhythm are those of the British infantry columns in the Boer War (1899-1902). The year after the British victory in South Africa, Kipling's poem appeared in a volume entitled The Five Nations.

The refrain "There's no discharge in the war!" echoes Ecclesiastes 8:8—"There is no man that hath power over the spirit to retain the spirit; neither hath he power in the day of death: and there is no discharge in the war." The bandoliers referred to in the fifth stanza are over-the-shoulder cartridge belts.

For a biographical note on Kipling, see page 85.

The Hell-Bound Train

ANONYMOUS

A Texas cowboy lay down on a barroom floor,
Having drunk so much he could drink no more;
So he fell asleep with a troubled brain
To dream that he rode on a hell-bound train.

The engine with murderous blood was damp
And was brilliantly lit with a brimstone lamp;
An imp, for fuel, was shoveling bones,
While the furnace rang with a thousand groans.

The boiler was filled with lager beer
And the devil himself was the engineer;
The passengers were a most motley crew—
Church member, atheist, Gentile, and Jew,

Rich men in broadcloth, beggars in rags,
Handsome young ladies, and withered old hags,
Yellow and black men, red, brown, and white,
All chained together—O God, what a sight!

While the train rushed on at an awful pace—
The sulphurous fumes scorched their hands and face;
Wider and wider the country grew,
As faster and faster the engine flew.

Louder and louder the thunder crashed
And brighter and brighter the lightning flashed;
Hotter and hotter the air became
Till the clothes were burned from each quivering
    frame.

And out of the distance there arose a yell,
"Ha, ha," said the devil, "we're nearing hell!"
Then oh, how the passengers all shrieked with pain
And begged the devil to stop the train.

But he capered about and danced for glee,
And laughed and joked at their misery.
"My faithful friends, you have done the work
And the devil never can a payday shirk.

"You've bullied the weak, you've robbed the poor,
The starving brother you've turned from the door;
You've laid up gold where the canker rust,
And have given free vent to your beastly lust.

"You've justice scorned, and corruption sown,
And trampled the laws of nature down.
You have drunk, rioted, cheated, plundered, and
    lied,
And mocked at God in your hell-born pride.

"You have paid full fare, so I'll carry you through,
For it's only right you should have your due.
Why, the laborer always expects his hire,
So I'll land you safe in the lake of fire,

"Where your flesh will waste in the flames that roar,
And my imps torment you forevermore."
Then the cowboy awoke with an anguished cry,
His clothes wet with sweat and his hair standing high.

Then he prayed as he never had prayed till that hour
To be saved from his sin and the demon's power;
And his prayers and his vows were not in vain,
For he never rode the hell-bound train.

This roaring vision of damnation is one of the many American and British poems which combine a speeding locomotive and imminent doom. Even the nightmare train of this poem has its cousins—"Asleep at the Switch," also anonymous, is perhaps the prime example. Other notable train poems are Eugene Hall's "The Engineer's Story," George R. Sims's "The Signal Box," Frank L. Stanton's "The Printer's 'Devil,' Jim," Bret Harte's "Guild's Signal," J. G. Whittier's "Conductor Bradley," and the song "Casey Jones."

Song of the Shirt

THOMAS HOOD (1799-1845)

With fingers weary and worn,
  With eyelids heavy and red,
A woman sat in unwomanly rags,
  Plying her needle and thread—
Stitch! stitch! stitch!
  In poverty, hunger and dirt,
And still with a voice of dolorous pitch
  She sang the "Song of the Shirt!"

"Work! work! work!
  While the cock is crowing aloof!
And work—work—work,
  Till the stars shine through the roof!
It's oh! to be a slave
  Along with the barbarous Turk,
Where a woman has never a soul to save,
  If this is Christian work!

"Work—work—work
  Till the brain begins to swim;
Work—work—work
  Till the eyes are heavy and dim!
Seam, and gusset, and band,
  Band, and gusset, and seam,
Till over the buttons I fall asleep,
  And sew them on in a dream!

"O men, with sisters dear!
O men, with mothers and wives!
It is not linen you're wearing out,
But human creatures' lives!
Stitch—stitch—stitch!
In poverty, hunger and dirt,—
Sewing at once, with a double thread,
A shroud as well as a shirt!

"But why do I talk of Death,—
That phantom of grisly bone?
I hardly fear his terrible shape,
It seems so like my own,—
It seems so like my own
Because of the fasts I keep;
O God! that bread should be so dear,
And flesh and blood so cheap!

"Work! work! work!
My labor never flags;
And what are its wages? A bed of straw,
A crust of bread—and rags,
That shattered roof—and this naked floor—
A table—a broken chair—
And a wall so blank, my shadow I thank
For sometimes falling there!

"Work—work—work!
From weary chime to chime!
Work—work—work!
As prisoners work for crime!

Band, and gusset, and seam,
  Seam, and gusset, and band,—
Till the heart is sick and the brain benumbed,
  As well as the weary hand.

"Work—work—work!
  In the dull December light!
And work—work—work!
  When the weather is warm and bright!
While underneath the eaves
  The brooding swallows cling,
As if to show me their sunny backs,
  And twit me with the spring.

"Oh, but to breathe the breath
  Of the cowslip and primrose sweet,—
With the sky above my head,
  And the grass beneath my feet!
For only one short hour
  To feel as I used to feel,
Before I knew the woes of want
  And the walk that costs a meal!

"Oh, but for one short hour,—
  A respite, however brief!
No blessed leisure for love or hope,
  But only time for grief!
A little weeping would ease my heart;
  But in their briny bed
My tears must stop, for every drop
  Hinders needle and thread!"

With fingers weary and worn,
　With eyelids heavy and red,
A woman sat in unwomanly rags,
　Plying her needle and thread,—
Stitch! stitch! stitch!
　In poverty, hunger and dirt;
And still with a voice of dolorous pitch—
Would that its tone could reach the rich!—
　She sang the "Song of the Shirt."

Thomas Hood wrote mostly humorous poems, despite a lifetime of poor health and money worries. Yet it is his serious verse for which he was held dear by his contemporaries and by readers of today.

"Song of the Shirt" and "Bridge of Sighs" show a marvelous compassion for the careworn. The popularity of "Song of the Shirt"—with its powerful extra line in the final stanza—actually inspired legislators to ease the working conditions of the poor "slop" seamstresses.

The Blind Men and the Elephant

JOHN GODFREY SAXE (1816-1887)

It was six men of Indostan
　　To learning much inclined,
Who went to see the Elephant
　　(Though all of them were blind),
That each by observation
　　Might satisfy his mind.

The *First* approached the Elephant,
　　And happening to fall
Against his broad and sturdy side,
　　At once began to bawl:
"God bless me! but the Elephant
　　Is very like a wall!"

The *Second*, feeling of the tusk,
  Cried, "Ho! what have we here
So very round and smooth and sharp?
  To me 'tis mighty clear
This wonder of an Elephant
  Is very like a spear!"

The *Third* approached the animal,
  And happening to take
The squirming trunk within his hands,
  Thus boldly up and spake:
"I see," quoth he, "the Elephant
  Is very like a snake!"

The *Fourth* reached out an eager hand,
  And felt about the knee.
"What most this wondrous beast is like
  Is mighty plain," quoth he;
"'Tis clear enough the Elephant
  Is very like a tree!"

The *Fifth* who chanced to touch the ear,
  Said: "E'en the blindest man
Can tell what this resembles most;
  Deny the fact who can,
This marvel of an Elephant
  Is very like a fan!"

The *Sixth* no sooner had begun
  About the beast to grope,

Than, seizing on the swinging tail
   That fell within his scope,
"I see," quoth he, "the Elephant
   Is very like a rope!"

And so these men of Indostan
   Disputed loud and long,
Each in his own opinion
   Exceeding stiff and strong,
Though each was partly in the right,
   And all were in the wrong!

THE MORAL:

So oft in theologic wars,
   The disputants, I ween,
Rail on in utter ignorance
   Of what each other mean,
And prate about an Elephant
   Not one of them has seen!

John Godfrey Saxe was born in Vermont, the son of a mill owner. He trained for the law, and subsequently served the public as a Superintendent of Schools, a State's Attorney, and a U. S. Customs Collector. As a sideline, he submitted humorous verses to the literary magazines of the day.

These poems—such as "Sonnet to a Clam," "The Briefless Barrister," and "Echo"—proved immensely popular. Saxe moved down to New York to hobnob with literati like himself, and soon became one of the most highly prized after-dinner speakers in town.

Barbara Frietchie

JOHN GREENLEAF WHITTIER (1807-1892)

Up from the meadows rich with corn,
Clear in the cool September morn,

The clustered spires of Frederick stand
Green-walled by the hills of Maryland.

Round about them orchards sweep,
Apple and peach tree fruited deep,

Fair as the garden of the Lord
To the eyes of the famished rebel horde,

On that pleasant morn of the early fall
When Lee marched over the mountain wall;

Over the mountains winding down,
Horse and foot, into Frederick town.

Forty flags with their silver stars,
Forty flags with their crimson bars,

Flapped in the morning wind: the sun
Of noon looked down, and saw not one.

Up rose old Barbara Frietchie then,
Bowed with her fourscore years and ten;

Bravest of all in Frederick town,
She took up the flag the men hauled down;

In her attic window the staff she set,
To show that one heart was loyal yet.

Up the street came the rebel tread.
Stonewall Jackson riding ahead.

Under his slouched hat left and right
He glanced; the old flag met his sight.

"Halt!"—the dust-brown ranks stood fast,
"Fire"—out blazed the rifle-blast.

It shivered the window, pane and sash;
It rent the banner with seam and gash.

She leaned far out on the window-sill,
And shook it forth with a royal will.

"Shoot, if you must, this old gray head,
But spare your country's flag," she said.

A shade of sadness, a blush of shame,
Over the face of the leader came;

The nobler nature within him stirred
To life at that woman's deed and word;

"Who touches a hair of yon gray head
Dies like a dog! March on!" he said.

Quick as it fell, from the broken staff
Dame Barbara snatched the silken scarf.

All day long through Frederick street
Sounded the tread of marching feet:

All day long that free flag tossed
Over the heads of the rebel host.

Ever its torn folds rose and fell
On the loyal winds that loved it well;

And through the hill-gaps sunset light
Shone over it with a warm good-night.

Barbara Frietchie's work is o'er,
And the Rebel rides on his raids no more.

Honor to her! and let a tear
Fall, for her sake, on Stonewall's bier.

Over Barbara Frietchie's grave,
Flag of Freedom and Union, wave!

Peace and order and beauty draw
Round thy symbol of light and law;

And ever the stars above look down
On thy stars below in Frederick town!

John Greenleaf Whittier, the "Poet Laureate of New England," was born to a poor Quaker family in Haverhill, Massachusetts. His first eighteen years were spent on the farm, and the only formal

education he was ever to have were the two terms he spent at Haverhill Academy—paid for with the savings he had collected from shoemaking.

Whittier published his first poem in William Lloyd Garrison's Newburyport Free Press. *He soon came under the influence of the abolitionist Garrison, and became one of the most outspoken proponents of the cause. As a poet, Whittier is best known for his poems of rural New England, particularly* Snowbound.

The hero of the poem above should have been Mrs. Mary A. Quantrell, not Barbara Frietchie. When Stonewall Jackson marched into Fredericksburg, Virginia, in 1862, it was the middle-aged Mrs. Quantrell who raised the Union flag at her window. Jackson's Confederates are reported to have saluted and said, "To you, madam, and not to your flag!" One week later, the ninety-six-year-old Mrs. Frietchie took a somewhat safer course by raising the Union flag as Federal troops passed by her house.

Charge of the Light Brigade

ALFRED TENNYSON (1809-1892)

Half a league, half a league,
Half a league onward,
All in the valley of Death
  Rode the six hundred.
"Forward, the Light Brigade!
Charge for the guns!" he said:
Into the valley of Death
  Rode the six hundred.

"Forward, the Light Brigade!"
Was there a man dismayed?
Not tho' the soldiers knew
  Some one had blundered:
Theirs not to make reply,
Theirs not to reason why,
Theirs but to do and die:
Into the valley of Death
  Rode the six hundred.

Cannon to right of them,
Cannon to left of them,
Cannon in front of them
  Volleyed and thunder'd;

Storm'd at with shot and shell,
Boldly they rode and well,
Into the jaws of Death,
Into the mouth of Hell,
  Rode the six hundred.

Flashed all their sabres bare,
Flashed as they turned in air,
Sab'ring the gunners there,
Charging an army, while
  All the world wondered:
Plunged in the battery smoke,
Right through the line they broke;
Cossack and Russian
Reeled from the sabre-stroke
  Shattered and sundered.
Then they rode back, but not—
  Not the six hundred.

Cannon to right of them,
Cannon to left of them,
Cannon behind them
  Volleyed and thundered;
Stormed at with shot and shell,
While horse and hero fell,
They that had fought so well
Came thro' the jaws of Death,
Back from the mouth of Hell,
All that was left of them,
  Left of six hundred.

When can their glory fade?
Oh, the wild charge they made!
  All the world wondered.
Honor the charge they made!
Honor the Light Brigade,
  Noble Six Hundred!

Alfred Tennyson typified the "Establishment" poet so unfashionable in our century. He was born into wealth, was declared a genius in his teens, became Queen Victoria's favorite poet, was elevated to the peerage, and finally, was laid to rest in Westminster Abbey. Even the most tragic event of his life—the death, at 23, of his Cambridge chum Arthur Henry Hallam—proved grist for his poetic mill: the magnificent In Memorian.

"The Charge of the Light Brigade" was provoked by the London Times *report of a disaster at Balaclava in the Crimea. Lord Lucan—the "some one" who "had blunder'd" of stanza 2, line 4—had ordered the 673 officers of the Light Brigade to hurl themselves at 12,000 powerfully armed Russians. That only 247 of the officers perished seems remarkable.*

Some of Tennyson's other great works are Idylls of the King, Morte d'Arthur, *"Ulysses,"* The Princess, *"Crossing the Bar," and* Maud.

The Man with the Hoe

EDWIN MARKHAM (1852-1940)

Bowed by the weight of centuries he leans
Upon his hoe and gazes on the ground,
The emptiness of ages in his face,
And on his back the burden of the world.
Who made him dead to rapture and despair,
A thing that grieves not and that never hopes,
Stolid and stunned, a brother to the ox?
Who loosened and let down this brutal jaw?
Whose was the hand that slanted back this brow?
Whose breath blew out the light within this brain?

Is this the Thing the Lord God made and gave
To have dominion over sea and land,
To trace the stars and search the heavens for power,
To feel the passion of Eternity?
Is this the Dream He dreamed who shaped the suns
And pillared the blue firmament with light?
Down all the stretch of hell to its last gulf
There is no shape more terrible than this—
More tongued with censure of the world's blind
    greed—
More filled with signs and portents for the soul—
More fraught with menace to the universe.

What gulfs between him and the seraphim!
Slaves of the wheel of labor, what to him

Are Plato and the swing of Pleiades?
What the long reaches of the peaks of song,
The rift of dawn, the reddening of the rose?
Through this dread shape the suffering ages look;
Time's tragedy is in that aching stoop;
Through this dread shape humanity betrayed,
Plundered, profaned, and disinherited,
Cried protest to the Judges of the World,
A protest that is also prophecy.

O masters, lords, and rulers in all lands,
Is this the handiwork you give to God,
This monstrous thing distorted and soul-quenched?
How will you ever straighten up this shape,
Touch it again with immortality;

Give back the upward looking and the light;
Rebuild in it the music and the dream;
Make right the immemorial infamies,
Perfidious wrongs, immedicable woes?

O masters, lords, and rulers in all lands,
How will the Future reckon with this Man?
How answer his brute question in that hour
When whirlwinds of rebellion shake the world?
How will it be with kingdoms and with kings—
With those who shaped him to the thing he is—
When this dumb Terror shall reply to God,
After the silence of the centuries?

*Edwin Markham was born in Oregon City, Oregon,
but grew up in California. After a few years of cow-
punching, he went to college and, upon graduation,
became a teacher. In his forty-seventh year, 1899, he
was inspired by Millet's painting* The Gleaners *to
write "The Man with the Hoe." Millet's bowed,
weary peasant became for Markham a symbol of the
degradation of all laborers. Immediately after its
publication in the San Francisco* Examiner,
*Markham's poem struck a responsive chord not only
in America, but throughout the Western world.*

*Although Markham continued to write verse, his
career was marked by only one other success—
"Lincoln, the Man of the People," published in 1901.
He spent the last four decades of his life in the East,
on New York's Staten Island.*

Nothing to Wear

WILLIAM ALLEN BUTLER (1825-1902)

Miss Flora McFlimsey, of Madison Square,
Has made three separate journeys to Paris,
And her father assures me, each time she was there,
That she and her friend Mrs. Harris
(Not the lady whose name is so famous in history,
But plain Mrs. H., without romance or mystery)
Spent six consecutive weeks without stopping
In one continuous round of shopping,—
Shopping alone, and shopping together,
At all hours of the day, and in all sorts of weather,—
For all manner of things that a woman can put
On the crown of her head or the sole of her foot,
Or wrap round her shoulders, or fit round her waist,
Or that can be sewed on, or pinned on, or laced,
Or tied on with a string, or stitched on with a bow,
In front or behind, above or below;
For bonnets, mantillas, capes, collars, and shawls;
Dresses for breakfasts and dinners and balls;
Dresses to sit in and stand in and walk in;
Dresses to dance in and flirt in and talk in;
Dresses in which to do nothing at all;
Dresses for winter, spring, summer, and fall;
All of them different in color and pattern,
Silk, muslin, and lace, crape, velvet, and satin,
Brocade, and broadcloth, and other material,
Quite as expensive and much more ethereal;

In short, for all things that could ever be thought of,
Or milliner, *modiste,* or tradesman be bought of,
From ten-thousand-francs robes to twenty-sous
frills;
In all quarters of Paris, and to every store,
While McFlimsey in vain stormed, scolded, and
swore,
They footed the streets, and he footed the bills.

The last trip, their goods shipped by the steamer
Arago,
Formed, McFlimsey declares, the bulk of her cargo,
Not to mention a quantity kept from the rest,
Sufficient to fill the largest-sized chest,
Which did not appear on the ship's manifest,
But for which the ladies themselves manifested
Such particular interest, that they invested
Their own proper persons in layers and rows
Of muslins, embroideries, worked underclothes,
Gloves, handkerchiefs, scarfs, and such trifles as
those;
Then, wrapped in great shawls, like Circassian
beauties,
Gave *good-by* to the ship, and *go-by* to the duties.
Her relations at home all marveled, no doubt
Miss Flora had grown so enormously stout
For an actual belle and a possible bride;
But the miracle ceased when she turned inside out,
And the truth came to light, and the dry-goods
beside,

Which, in spite of collector and custom-house sentry,
Had entered the port without any entry.

And yet, though scarce three months have passed
    since the day
This merchandise went, on twelve carts, up
    Broadway,
This same Miss McFlimsey, of Madison Square,
The last time we met was in utter despair,
Because she had nothing whatever to wear!

NOTHING TO WEAR! Now, as this is a true ditty,
    I do not assert—this, you know, is between us—
That she's in a state of absolute nudity,
    Like Powers' Greek Slave, or the Medici Venus;
But I do mean to say, I have heard her declare,
    When, at the same moment, she had on a dress
    Which cost five hundred dollars, and not a cent
    less
    And jewelry worth ten times more, I should
    guess,
That she had not a thing in the wide world to wear!

I should mention just here, that out of Miss Flora's
Two hundred and fifty or sixty adorers,
I had just been selected as he who should throw all
The rest in the shade, by the gracious bestowal
On myself, after twenty or thirty rejections,
Of those fossil remains which she called her "affec-
    tions,"

And that rather decayed, but well-known work of
    art,
Which Miss Flora persisted in styling "her heart."

So we were engaged. Our troth had been plighted,
Not by moonbeam or starbeam, by fountain or
    grove,
But in a front parlor, most brilliantly lighted,
Beneath the gas-fixtures we whispered our love.
Without any romance or raptures or sighs,
Without any tears in Miss Flora's blue eyes,
Or blushes, or transports, or such silly actions,
It was one of the quietest business transactions,
With a very small sprinkling of sentiment, if any,
And a very large diamond imported by Tiffany.
On her virginal lips while I printed a kiss,
She exclaimed, as a sort of parenthesis,
And by way of putting me quite at my ease,
"You know, I'm to polka as much as I please.
And flirt when I like,—now, stop, don't you speak,—
And you must not come here more than twice in the
    week,
Or talk to me either at party or ball,
But always be ready to come when I call;
So don't prose to me about duty and stuff,
If we don't break this off, there will be time enough
For that sort of thing; but the bargain must be
That, as long as I choose, I am perfectly free,
For this is a sort of engagement, you see,
Which is binding on you but not binding on me."

Well, having thus wooed Miss McFlimsey and gained
    her,
With the silks, crinolines, and hoops that contained
    her;

I had, as I thought, a contingent remainder
At least in the property, and the best right
To appear as its escort by day and by night;
And it being the week of the Stuckups' grand ball,—
    Their cards had been out for a fortnight or so,
    And set all the Avenue on the tiptoe,—
I considered it only my duty to call,
    And see if Miss Flora intended to go.
I found her,—as ladies are apt to be found,
When the time intervening between the first sound
Of the bell and the visitor's entry is shorter
Than usual,—I found—I won't say, I caught her,—
Intent on the pier-glass, undoubtedly meaning
To see if perhaps it didn't need cleaning.
She turned as I entered,—"Why, Harry, you sinner,
I thought that you went to the Flashers' to dinner!"
"So I did," I replied; "but the dinner is swallowed
    And digested, I trust, for 'tis now nine and more,
So being relieved from that duty, I followed
    Inclination, which led me, you see, to your door;
And now will your ladyship so condescend
As just to inform me if you intend
Your beauty and graces and presence to lend
(All of which, when I own, I hope no one will
    borrow)
To the Stuckups', whose party, you know, is to-
    morrow?"

The fair Flora looked up with a pitiful air,
And answered quite promptly, "Why, Harry, *mon
    cher*,

I should like above all things to go with you there;
But really and truly—I've nothing to wear."

"Nothing to wear! go just as you are;
Wear the dress you have on, and you'll be by far,
I engage, the most bright and particular star
    On the Stuckup horizon"—I stopped—for her
    eye,
Notwithstanding this delicate onset of flattery,
Opened on me at once a most terrible battery
    Of scorn and amazement. She made no reply,
But gave a slight turn to the end of her nose
    (That pure Grecian feature), as much as to say,
"How absurd that any sane man should suppose
That a lady would go to a ball in the clothes,
    No matter how fine, that she wears every day!"

So I ventured again: "Wear your crimson brocade,"
(Second turn-up of nose)—"That's too dark by a
    shade."
"Your blue silk"—"That's too heavy." "Your pink"—
    "That's too light."
"Wear tulle over satin"—"I can't endure white."
"Your rose-colored, then, the best of the batch"—
"I haven't a thread of point lace to match."
"Your brown *moire antique*"—"Yes, and look like a
    Quaker."
"The pearl-colored"—"I would, but that plaguey
    dressmaker

Has had it a week." "Then that exquisite lilac
In which you would melt the heart of a Shylock."
(Here the nose took again the same elevation)—
"I wouldn't wear that for the whole of creation."
      "Why not? It's my fancy, there's nothing could
      strike it
As more *comme il faut*"—"Yes, but, dear me! that
      lean
      Sophronia Stuckup has got one just like it,
And I won't appear dressed like a chit of sixteen."
"Then that splendid purple, that sweet Mazarine,
That superb *point d'aiguille*, that imperial green,
That zephyr-like tarlatan, that rich *grenadine*"—
"Not one of all which is fit to be seen,"
Said the lady, becoming excited and flushed.
"Then wear," I exclaimed, in a tone which quite
      crushed
      Opposition, "that gorgeous *toilette* which you
      sported
In Paris last spring, at the grand presentation,
When you quite turned the head of the head of the
      nation;
      And by all the grand court were so very much
      courted."
      The end of the nose was portentously tipped up,
And both the bright eyes shot forth indignation,
As she burst upon me with the fierce exclamation,
"I have worn it three times at the least calculation,
      And that and the most of my dresses are ripped
      up!"

Here I ripped *out* something, perhaps rather rash,
    Quite innocent, though; but, to use an expression
More striking than classic, it "settled my hash,"
    And proved very soon the last act of our session.
"Fiddlesticks, it is, sir? I wonder the ceiling
Doesn't fall down and crush you—oh! you men have
    no feeling;
You selfish, unnatural, illiberal creatures,
Who set yourselves up as patterns and preachers,
Your silly pretense,—why, what a mere guess it is!
Pray, what do you know of a woman's necessities!
I have told you and shown you I've nothing to wear,
And it's perfectly plain you not only don't care,
But you do not believe me" (here the nose went still
    higher).
"I suppose, if you dared, you would call me a liar.
Our engagement is ended, sir—yes, on the spot;
You're a brute and a monster, and—I don't know
    what."
I mildly suggested the words—Hottentot,
Pickpocket, and cannibal, Tartar, and thief,
As gentle expletives which might give relief;
But this only proved as spark to the powder,
And the storm I had raised came faster and louder;
It blew and it rained, thundered, lightened, and
    hailed
Interjections, verbs, pronouns, till language quite
    failed
To express the abusive, and then its arrears
Were brought up all at once by a torrent of tears,

And my last faint, despairing attempt at an obs-
Ervation was lost in a tempest of sobs.

Well, I felt for the lady, and felt for my hat, too,
Improvised on the crown of the latter a tattoo,
In lieu of expressing the feelings which lay
Quite too deep for words, as Wordsworth would say;
Then, without going through the form of a bow,
Found myself in the entry—I hardly knew how,—
On doorstep and sidewalk, past lamp-post and
    square,
At home and up stairs, in my own easy-chair;
    Poked my feet into slippers, my fire into blaze,
And said to myself, as I lit my cigar,
Supposing a man had the wealth of the Czar
    Of the Russias to boot, for the rest of his days,
On the whole, do you think he would have much to
    spare,
If he married a woman with nothing to wear?

Since that night, taking pains that it should not be
  bruited
Abroad in society, I've instituted
A course of inquiry, extensive and thorough
On this vital subject, and find, to my horror,
That the fair Flora's case is by no means surprising,
  But that there exists the greatest distress
In our female community, solely arising
  From this unsupplied destitution of dress,
Whose unfortunate victims are filling the air
With the pitiful wail of "Nothing to Wear."
Researches in some of the "Upper Ten" districts
Reveal the most painful and startling statistics,
Of which let me mention only a few:
In one single house, on Fifth Avenue,
Three young ladies were found, all below twenty-
  two,
Who have been three whole weeks without anything
  new
In the way of flounced silks, and, thus left in the
  lurch,
Are unable to go to ball, concert, or church.
In another large mansion, near the same place,
Was found a deplorable, heartrending case
Of entire destitution of Brussels point lace.
In a neighboring block there was found, in three
  calls,
Total want, long continued, of camel's-hair shawls;
And a suffering family, whose case exhibits
The most pressing need of real ermine tippets;

One deserving young lady almost unable
To survive for the want of a new Russian sable;
Another confined to the house, when it's windier
Than usual, because her shawl isn't India.
Still another, whose tortures have been most terrific
Ever since the sad loss of the steamer *Pacific,*
In which were engulfed, not friend or relation
(For whose fate she perhaps might have found
    consolation
Or borne it, at least, with serene resignation),
But the choicest assortment of French sleeves and
    collars
Ever sent out from Paris, worth thousands of dollars,
And all as to style most *recherché* and rare,
The want of which leaves her with nothing to wear,
And renders her life so drear and dyspeptic
That she's quite a recluse, and almost a skeptic;
For she touchingly says that this sort of grief
Cannot find in Religion the slightest relief,
And Philosophy has not a maxim to spare
For the victims of such overwhelming despair.
But the saddest by far of all these sad features
Is the cruelty practised upon the poor creatures
By husbands and fathers, real Bluebeards and
    Timons,
Who resist the most touching appeals made for
    diamonds
By their wives and their daughters, and leave them
    for days
Unsupplied with new jewelry, fans, or bouquets,

Even laugh at their miseries whenever they have a
    chance,
And deride their demands as useless extravagance;
One case of a bride was brought to my view,
Too sad for belief, but, alas! 'twas too true,
Whose husband refused, as savage as Charon,
To permit her to take more than ten trunks to Sharon.
The consequence was, that when she got there,
At the end of three weeks she had nothing to wear,
And when she proposed to finish the season
    At Newport, the monster refused out and out,
For his infamous conduct alleging no reason,
    Except that the waters were good for his gout.
Such treatment as this was too shocking, of course,
And proceedings are now going on for divorce.

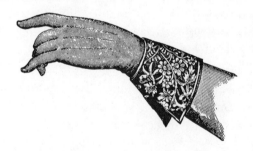

But why harrow the feelings by lifting the curtain
From these scenes of woe? Enough, it is certain,
Has here been disclosed to stir up the pity
Of every benevolent heart in the city,
And spur up Humanity into a canter
To rush and relieve these sad cases instanter.

Won't somebody, moved by this touching descrip-
    tion,
Come forward to-morrow and head a subscription?
Won't some kind philanthropist, seeing that aid is
So needed at once by these indigent ladies,
Take charge of the matter? Or won't Peter Cooper
The corner-stone lay of some splendid super-
Structure, like that which to-day links his name
In the Union unending of honor and fame;
And found a new charity just for the care
Of these unhappy women with nothing to wear,
Which, in view of the cash which would daily be
    claimed,
The *Laying-out* Hospital well might be named?
Won't Stewart, or some of our dry-goods importers,
Take a contract for clothing our wives and our
    daughters?
Or, to furnish the cash to supply these distresses,
And life's pathway strew with shawls, collars, and
    dresses,
Ere the want of them makes it much rougher and
    thornier,
Won't some one discover a new California?

Oh, ladies, dear ladies, the next sunny day
Please trundle your hoops just out of Broadway,
From its whirl and its bustle, its fashion and pride,
And the temples of Trade which tower on each side,
To the alleys and lanes, where Misfortune and Guilt
Their children have gathered, their city have built;

Where Hunger and Vice, like twin beasts of prey,
  Have hunted their victims to gloom and despair;
Raise the rich, dainty dress, and the fine broidered
  skirt,
Pick your delicate way through the dampness and
  dirt,
    Grope through the dark dens, climb the rickety
    stair
To the garret, where wretches, the young and the
  old,
Half-starved and half-naked, lie crouched from the
  cold.
See those skeleton limbs, those frost-bitten feet,
All bleeding and bruised by the stones of the street;
Hear the sharp cry of childhood, the deep groans that
  swell
    From the poor dying creature who writhes on
    the floor,
Hear the curses that sound like the ees of Hell,
    As you sicken and shudder and fly from the
    door;
Then home to your wardrobes, and say, if you
  dare,—
Spoiled children of Fashion,—you've nothing to
  wear!

And oh, if perchance there should be a sphere
Where all is made right which so puzzles us here,
Where the glare and the glitter and tinsel of Time
Fade and die in the light of that region sublime,

Where the soul, disenchanted of flesh and of sense,
Unscreened by its trappings and shows and pretense,
Must be clothed for the life and the service above,
With purity, truth, faith, meekness, and love;
O daughters of Earth! foolish virgins, beware!
Lest in that upper realm you have nothing to wear!

*William Allen Butler was a lawyer first, a poet
second; he versified only as much as his profession
allowed him. While "Nothing to Wear" was an
immediate sensation upon its publication in 1857, he
produced little else of note. Indeed, even during his
lifetime, his principal fame was as a lawyer.*

*Nonetheless, "Nothing to Wear" remains a popular
choice of orators, and "one-poem poets" are not to be
sneered at. Their ranks include such as Clement C.
Moore ("A Visit from St. Nicholas"), Ernest L.
Thayer ("Casey at the Bat"), Adelaide Proctor ("The
Lost Chord"), and Samuel Woodworth ("The Old
Oaken Bucket").*

Shameful Death

WILLIAM MORRIS (1834-1896)

There were four of us about that bed;
   The mass-priest knelt at the side,
I and his mother stood at the head,
   Over his feet lay the bride;
We were quite sure that he was dead,
   Though his eyes were open wide.

He did not die in the night,
   He did not die in the day,
But in the morning twilight
   His spirit pass'd away,
When neither sun nor moon was bright,
   And the trees were merely grey.

He was not slain with the sword,
   Knight's axe, or the knightly spear,
Yet spoke he never a word
   After he came in here;
I cut away the cord
   From the neck of my brother dear.

He did not strike one blow,
   For the recreants came behind,
In a place where the hornbeams grow,
   A path right hard to find,

For the hornbeam boughs swing so,
    That the twilight makes it blind.

They lighted a great torch then,
    When his arms were pinion'd fast,
Sir John the knight of the Fen,
    Sir Guy of the Dolorous Blast,
With knights threescore and ten,
    Hung brave Lord Hugh at last.

I am threescore and ten,
    And my hair is all turn'd grey,
But I met Sir John of the Fen
    Long ago on a summer day,
And am glad to think of the moment when
    I took his life away.

I am threescore and ten,
    And my strength is mostly pass'd,
But long ago I and my men,
    When the sky was overcast,
And the smoke roll'd over the reeds of the fen,
    Slew Guy of the Dolorous Blast.

And now, knights all of you,
    I pray you pray for Sir Hugh,
A good knight and a true,
    And for Alice, his wife, pray too.

William Morris was, to mix eras, the Renaissance Man of Victorian England. He was a consummate artist, printer, architect, designer, and poet. As a boy, he read the Waverly novels of Sir Walter Scott, and developed a life-long love for the medieval. He studied first architecture, then painting; for relaxation, he dabbled in poetry. His first volume of verse, The Defence of Guenevere, and Other Poems (1858) included "Shameful Death."

For the next seven years, Morris abandoned poetry to embark on a grand project to elevate the artistic quality of merchandise intended for common use. He and his Pre-Raphaelite friends started workshops for the production of such articles as furniture, wallpaper, cloth, and glassware. This conscious attempt to return to the medieval guild system had some notable successes.

In his later years, Morris delved into Norse and Icelandic folklore, socialism, and book design—via the magnificent Kelmscott Press, which he managed from his country estate in Hammersmith. Morris designed the type, the bindings, and the distinctive page borders that make Kelmscott books collectors' treasures.

In "Shameful Death,".the only word which might give pause is "hornbeam"—a tree with a smooth gray bark and leaves like those of the beech.

The Vampire

RUDYARD KIPLING (1865-1936)

A fool there was and he made his prayer
(Even as you and I!)
To a rag and a bone and a hank of hair,
(We called her the woman who did not care),
But the fool he called her his lady fair—
(Even as you and I!)

O, the years we waste and the tears we waste,
And the work of our head and hand
Belong to the woman who did not know
(And now we know that she never could know)
And did not understand!

A fool there was and his goods he spent,
(Even as you and I!)
Honour and faith and a sure intent
(And it wasn't the least what the lady meant),
But a fool must follow his natural bent
(Even as you and I!)

Oh, the toil we lost and the spoil we lost
And the excellent things we planned
Belong to the woman who didn't know why
(And now we know that she never knew why)
And did not understand!

The fool was stripped to his foolish hide,
(Even as you and I!)
Which she might have seen when she threw him
    aside—
(But it isn't on record the lady tried)
So some of him lived but the most of him died—
(Even as you and I!)

"And it isn't the shame and it isn't the blame
That stings like a white-hot brand—
It's coming to know that she never knew why
(Seeing, at last, she could never know why)
And never could understand!"

Although feminists will find little to laud in this
recitation, it is a powerfully rhythmic poem. The
baldly misogynist feelings voiced in this poem
elicited "A Woman's Answer to 'The Vampire'" from
Felicia Blake, which concludes:

And it isn't the ache of the heart, or its break,
That stings like a white-hot brand—
It's learning to know that she raised the rod,
And bent her head to kiss the rod
For one who would not understand

In a similar vein, Kipling also wrote "The Female
of the Species," with its famous refrain of "For the
female of the species is more deadly than the male."
For a biographical note on Kipling, see page 85.

Horatius

THOMAS BABINGTON MACAULAY (1800-1859)

Lars Porsena of Clusium
　By the Nine Gods he swore
That the great house of Tarquin
　Should suffer wrong no more.
By the Nine Gods he swore it,
　And named a trysting day,
And bade his messengers ride forth,
East and west and south and north,
　To summon his array.

East and west and south and north
　The messengers ride fast,
And tower and town and cottage
　Have heard the trumpet's blast.
Shame on the false Etruscan
　Who lingers in his home
When Porsena of Clusium
　Is on the march for Rome.

The horsemen and the footmen
　Are pouring in amain,
From many a stately market-place;
　From many a fruitful plain;
From many a lonely hamlet,
　Which, hid by beech and pine,
Like an eagle's nest, hangs on the crest
　Of purple Apennine.

And now hath every city
   Sent up her tale of men;
The foot are fourscore thousand,
   The horse are thousands ten.
Before the gates of Sutrium
   Is met the great array.
A proud man was Lars Porsena
   Upon the trysting day.

For all the Etruscan armies
   Were ranged beneath his eye,
And many a banished Roman,
   And many a stout ally;
And with a mighty following
   To join the muster came
The Tusculan Mamilius,
   Prince of the Latian name.

But by the yellow Tiber
  Was tumult and affright:
From all the spacious champaign
  To Rome men took their flight.
A mile around the city,
  The throng stopped up the ways;
A fearful sight it was to see
  Through two long nights and days.

For aged folk on crutches,
  And women great with child,
Wnd mothers sobbing over babes
  That clung to them and smiled,
And sick men borne in litters
  High on the necks of slaves,
And troops of sun-burned husbandmen
  With reaping-hooks and staves.

And droves of mules and asses
  Laden with skins of wine,
And endless flocks of goats and sheep,
  And endless herds of kine,
And endless trains of wagons
  That creaked beneath the weight
Of corn-sacks and of household goods,
  Choked every roaring gate.

Now from the rock Tarpeian,
  Could the wan burghers spy
The line of blazing villages
  Red in the midnight sky.

The Fathers of the City,
    They sat all night and day,
For every hour some horseman came
    With tidings of dismay.

To eastward and to westward
    Have spread the Tuscan bands;
Nor house, nor fence, nor dovecote
    In Crustumerium stands.
Verbenna down to Ostia
    Hath wasted all the plain;
Astur hath stormed Janiculum,
    And the stout guards are slain.

I wis, in all the Senate,
    There was no heart so bold,
But sore it ached, and fast it beat,
    When that ill news was told.
Forthwith up rose the Consul,
    Up rose the Fathers all;
In haste they girded up their gowns,
    And hied them to the wall.

They held a council standing
    Before the River-gate;
Short time was there, ye well may guess,
    For musing or debate.
Out spake the Consul roundly:
    "The bridge must straight go down;
For, since Janiculum is lost,
    Naught else can save the town."

Just then a scout came flying,
  All wild with haste and fear:
"To arms! to arms! Sir Consul;
  Lars Porsena is here."
On the low hills to westward
  The Consul fixed his eye,
And saw the swarthy storm of dust
  Rise fast along the sky.

And nearer fast and nearer
  Doth the red whirlwind come;
And louder still, and still more loud
From underneath that rolling cloud,
Is heard the trumpet's war-note proud,
  The trampling, and the hum.
And plainly and more plainly
  Now through the gloom appears,
Far to left and far to right,
In broken gleams of dark-blue light,
The long array of helmets bright,
  The long array of spears.

And plainly and more plainly
  Now might the burghers know,
By port and vest, by horse and crest,
  Each warlike Lucomo.
There Cilnius of Arretium
  On his fleet roan was seen;
And Astur of the four-fold shield,
Girt with the brand none else may wield,

Tolumnius with the belt of gold,
And dark Verbenna from the hold
　　By reedy Thrasymene.

And the Consul's brow was sad,
　　And the Consul's speech was low,
And darkly looked he at the wall,
　　And darkly at the foe.
"Their van will be upon us
　　Before the bridge goes down;
And if they once may win the bridge,
　　What hope to save the town?"

Then out spake brave Horatius,
　　The Captain of the gate:
"To every man upon this earth
　　Death cometh soon or late.
And how can man die better
　　Than facing fearful odds,
For the ashes of his fathers
　　And the temples of his Gods!

"Hew down the bridge, Sir Consul,
　　With all the speed ye may;
I, with two more to help me,
　　Will hold the foe in play.
In yon strait path a thousand
　　May well be stopped by three.
Now who will stand on either hand,
　　And keep the bridge with me?"

Then out spake Spurius Lartius;
  A Ramnian proud was he:
"Lo, I will stand at thy right hand,
  And keep the bridge with thee."
And out spake strong Herminius;
  Of Titian blood was he:
"I will abide on they left side,
  And keep the bridge with thee."

"Horatius," quoth the Consul,
  "As thou sayest, so let it be."
And straight against that great array
  Forth went the dauntless Three.
For Romans in Rome's quarrel
  Spared neither land nor gold,
Nor son nor wife, nor limb nor life,
  In the brave days of old.

Now while the Three were tightening
    Their harness on their backs,
The Consul was the foremost man
    To take in hand an axe:
And Fathers mixed with Commons
    Seized hatchet, bar, and crow,
And smote upon the planks above,
    And loosed the props below.

Meanwhile the Tuscan army,
    Right glorious to behold,
Came flashing back the noonday light,
Rank behind rank, like surges bright
    Of a broad sea of gold.
Four hundred trumpets sounded
    A peal of warlike glee,
As that great host, with measured tread,
And spears advanced, and ensigns spread,
Rolled slowly towards the bridge's head,
    Where stood the dauntless Three.

The Three stood calm and silent
    And looked upon the foes,
And a great shout of laughter
    From all the vanguard rose:
And forth three chiefs came spurring
    Before that deep array;
To earth they sprang, their swords they drew,
And lifted high their shields, and flew
    To win the narrow way;

Aunus from green Tifernum,
   Lord of the Hill of Vines;
And Seius, whose eight hundred slaves
   Sicken in Ilva's mines;
And Picus, long to Clusium
   Vassal in peace and war,
Who led to fight his Umbrian powers
From that gray crag where, girt with towers,
The fortress of Nequinum lowers
   O'er the pale waves of Nar.

Stout Lartius hurled down Aunus
   Into the stream beneath:
Herminius struck at Seius,
   And clove him to the teeth:
At Picus brave Horatius
   Darted one fiery thrust;
And the proud Umbrian's gilded arms
   Clashed in the bloody dust.

Then Ocnus of Falerii
   Rushed on the Roman Three;
And Lausulus of Urgo,
   The rover of the sea;
And Aruns of Volsinium,
   Who slew the great wild boar,
The great wild boar that had his den
Amidst the reeds of Cosa's fen,
And wasted fields, and slaughtered men,
   Along Albinia's shore.

Herminius smote down Aruns:
    Lartius laid Ocnus low:
Right to the heart of Lausulus
    Horatius sent a blow.
"Lie there," he cried, "fell pirate!
    No more, aghast and pale,
From Ostia's walls the crowd shall mark
The track of thy destroying bark.
No more Campania's hinds shall fly
To woods and caverns when they spy
    Thy thrice accursed sail."

But now no sound of laughter
    Was heard among the foes.
A wild and wrathful clamor
    From all the vanguard rose.
Six spears' lengths from the entrance
    Halted that deep array,
And for a space no man came forth
    To win the narrow way.

But hark! the cry is Astur:
    And lo! the ranks divide;
And the great Lord of Luna
    Comes with his stately stride.
Upon his ample shoulders
    Clangs loud the four-fold shield,
And in his hand he shakes the brand
    Which none but he can wield.

He smiled on those bold Romans
  A smile serene and high;
He eyed the flinching Tuscans,
  And scorn was in his eye.
Quoth he, "The she-wolf's litter
  Stand savagely at bay:
But will ye dare to follow,
  If Astur clears the way?"

Then, whirling up his broadsword
  With both hands to the height,
He rushed against Horatius,
  And smote with all his might.
With shield and blade Horatius
  Right deftly turned the blow.
The blow, though turned, came yet too nigh;
It missed his helm, but gashed his thigh:
The Tuscans raised a joyful cry
  To see the red blood flow.

He reeled, and on Herminius
  He leaned one breathing-space;
Then, like a wild cat mad with wounds,
  Sprang right at Astur's face.
Through teeth, and skull, and helmet,
  So fierce a thrust he sped,
The good sword stood a hand-breadth out
  Behind the Tuscan's head.

And the great Lord of Luna
    Fell at that deadly stroke,
As falls on Mount Alvernus
    A thunder-smitten oak.
Far o'er the crashing forest
    The giant arms lie spread;
And the pale augurs, muttering low,
    Gaze on the blasted head.

On Astur's throat Horatius
    Right firmly pressed his heels,
And thrice and four times tugged amain,
    Ere he wrenched out the steel.
"And see," he cried, "the welcome,
    Fair guests, that waits you here!
What noble Lucomo comes next,
    To taste our Roman cheer?"

But at this haughty challenge
    A sullen murmur ran,
Mingled of wrath, and shame, and dread,
    Along that glittering van.
There lacked not men of prowess,
    Nor men of lordly race;
For all Etruria's noblest
    Were round the fatal place.

But all Etruria's noblest
    Felt their hearts sink to see
On the earth the bloody corpses,
    In the path the dauntless Three:

And, from the ghastly entrance
    Where those bold Romans stood,
All shrank, like boys who unaware,
Ranging the wods to start a hare,
Come to the mouth of the dark lair
Where, growling low, a fierce old bear
    Lies amidst bones and blood.

Was none who would be foremost
    To lead such dire attack;
But those behind cried "Forward!"
    And those before cried "Back!"
And backward now and forward
    Wavers the deep array;
And on the tossing sea of steel,
To and fro the standards reel;
And the victorious trumpet-peal
    Dies fitfully away.

But meanwhile axe and lever
    Have manfully been plied,
And now the bridge hangs tottering
    Above the boiling tide.
"Come back, come back, Horatius!"
    Loud cried the Fathers all.
"Back, Lartius! back, Herminius!
    Back, ere the ruin fall!"

Back darted Spurius Lartius;
    Herminius darted back:

And, as they passed, beneath their feet
    They felt the timbers crack.
But when they turned their faces,
    And on the farther shore
Saw brave Horatius stand alone,
    They would have crossed once more.

But with a crash like thunder
    Fell every loosened beam,
And, like a dam, the mighty wreck
    Lay right athwart the stream:
And a long shout of triumph
    Rose from the walls of Rome,
As to the highest turret-tops
    Was splashed the yellow foam.

And, like a horse unbroken
    When first he feels the rein,
The furious river struggled hard,
    And tossed his tawny mane,
And burst the curb, and bounded,
    Rejoicing to be free,
And whirling down, in fierce career,
Battlement, and plank, and pier,
    Rushed headlong to the sea.

Alone stood brave Horatius,
    But constant still in mind;
Thrice thirty thousand foes before,
    And the broad flood behind.

"Down with him!" cried false Sextus,
  With a smile on his pale face.
"Now yield thee," cried Lars Porsena,
  "Now yield thee to our grace."

Round turned he, as not deigning
  Those craven ranks to see;
Naught spake he to Lars Porsena,
  To Sextus naught spake he:
But he saw on Palatinus
  The white porch of his home;
And he spake to the noble river
  That rolls by the towers of Rome.

"Oh, Tiber! Father Tiber!
  To whom the Romans pray,
A Roman's life, a Roman's arms,
  Take thou in charge this day!"
So he spake, and speaking sheathed
  The good sword by his side,
And with his harness on his back,
  Plunged headlong in the tide.

No sound of joy or sorrow
  Was heard from either bank;
But friends and foes in dumb surprise,
With parted lips and straining eyes,
  Stood gazing where he sank;

And when above the surges
　　They saw his crest appear,
All Rome sent forth a rapturous cry,
And even the ranks of Tuscany
　　Could scarce forbear to cheer.

But fiercely ran the current,
　　Swollen high by months of rain:
And fast his blood was flowing;
　　And he was sore in pain,
And heavy with his armor,
　　And spent with changing blows:
And oft they thought him sinking,
　　But still again he rose.

Never, I ween, did swimmer,
　　In such an evil case,
Struggle through such a raging flood
　　Safe to the landing-place:
But his limbs were borne up bravely
　　By the brave heart within,
And our good Father Tiber
　　Bare bravely up his chin.

"Curse on him!" quoth false Sextus:
　　"Will not the villain drown?
But for this stay, ere close of day
　　We should have sacked the town!"
"Heaven help him!" quoth Lars Porsena,
　　"And bring him safe to shore;

For such a gallant feat of arms
    Was never seen before."

And now he feels the bottom;
    Now on dry earth he stands;
Now round him throng the Fathers
    To press his gory hands;
And now, with shouts and clapping,
    And noise of weeping loud,
He enters through the River-gate,
    Borne by the joyous crowd.

They gave him of the corn-land
    That was of public right
As much as two strong oxen
    Could plough from morn till night;
And they made a molten image,
    And set it up on high,
And there it stands unto this day
    To witness if I lie.

It stands in the Comitium,
    Plain for all folk to see;
Horatius in his harness,
    Halting upon one knee:
And underneath is written,
    In letters all of gold,
How valiantly he kept the bridge
    In the brave days of old.

Thomas Babington Macaulay was born in Leicestershire and educated at Cambridge. He began to write regularly for the prestigious Edinburgh Review *in 1825, and five years later was elected to Parliament. There, for much of the rest of his life, he was to serve the nation and the Whig party with distinction. Among the government posts he held were Secretary of War and Paymaster of the Forces. While serving the East India Company from 1834 to 1838, he reformed the colony's educational system and set down a legal code. In 1857, Queen Victoria named him Baron Macaulay of Rothley.*

As a poet, Macaulay is known primarily for "Horatius," "Virginia," and "The Armada." All three appeared in Lays of Ancient Rome *(1842, 1848), the only volume of verse he ever published. It is as a historian that Macaulay won his principal fame. His masterpiece is the* History of England from the Accession of James II *in five volumes.*

"Horatius," the longest recitation in this book, is in fact far longer than the abridged version printed here. It is one of the most rousing heroic poems in the English language.

In Hardin County

LULU E. THOMPSON (1839-1916)

With flintlocked guns and polished stocks,
Knee breeches and long homespun socks,
On morning of St. Valentine
Two hunters met in 1809.
Across the line from Illinois;
They stopped their mules and voiced their joy.

"Why, Ben, it's been quite a spell
Since I've seen you. The folks all well?
Bring any news from up near town?"
"Why, yes. D'you know John Ezry Brown?
They say that he's a-goin' down
To Washington in all the din
To see Jim Madison sworn in.

"And this young feller Bonaparte
    That's fightin' cross the sea,
Is slicin' Europe all to bits.

Least that's what they're a-tellin' me."
"Wal, wal, nice day, kinda breezy
This mule's gettin' quite uneasy.

"Now come and see us some time, do,
And bring the gals and Hepsy, too."
"Yes, some fine day we'll be along,
Got any news to send along?"

"No, nothin' worth a tinker's song.
There's nothin' happens here near me,
Doggondest place you ever see.

"Tom Lincoln lives right over there,
In that log cabin, bleak and bare,
They say they have a little babe,
I understand they've named him 'Abe.'
Yes, Sally said just 'tother day,
That nothin' happens down this way."

Nothing is known of the author of this rustic American ballad. Of the two hunters who stop to pass the time of day, Ben—who lives "up near town"—has all the news from far-off places. The other hunter, who lives in the backwoods of Hardin County, Kentucky, hasn't got any news "worth a tinker's song"—just that the Lincolns have had a baby boy named Abe. With the benefit of hindsight, readers can weigh this "trivial" piece of news against Ben's reports of Madison and Bonaparte.

Hardin County, Lincoln's birthplace, is today known as Larue County.

The Stone

W.W. GIBSON (1878-1962)

"And you will cut a stone for him,
To set above his head?
And will you cut a stone for him—
A stone for him?" she said.

Three days before, a splintered rock
Had struck her lover dead—
Had struck him in the quarry dead,
Where, careless of the warning call,
He loitered, while the shot was fired—
A lively stripling, brave and tall,
And sure of all his heart desired . . .
A flash, a shock,
A rumbling fall . . .
And, broken 'neath the broken rock,
A lifeless heap, with face of clay;
And still as any stone he lay,
With eyes that saw the end of all.

I went to break the news to her;
And I could hear my own heart beat
With dread of what my lips might say
But, some poor fool had sped before;
And flinging wide her father's door,
Had blurted out the news to her,
Had struck her lover dead for her,

Had struck the girl's heart dead in her,
Had struck life lifeless at a word,
And dropped it at her feet:
Then hurried on his witless way,
Scarce knowing she had heard.

And when I came, she stood alone,
A woman turned to stone:
And, though no word at all she said,
I knew that all was known.
Because her heart was dead,
She did not sigh nor moan,
His mother wept;
She could not weep.
Her lover slept:
She could not sleep.
Three days, three nights,
She did not stir:
Three days, three nights,
Were one to her,
Who never closed her eyes
From sunset to sunrise,
From dawn to evenfall:
Her tearless, staring eyes,
That seeing naught, saw all.

The fourth night when I came from work,
I found her at my door.
"And will you cut a stone for him?"
She said: and spoke no more:

But followed me, as I went in,
And sank upon a chair;
And fixed her gray eyes on my face,
With still, unseeing stare.
And, as she waited patiently,
I could not bear to feel
Those still, gray eyes that followed me,
Those eyes that plucked the heart from me,
Those eyes that sucked the breath from me
And curdled the warm blood in me,
Those eyes that cut me to the bone,
And pierced my marrow like cold steel.

And so I rose, and sought a stone;
And cut it, smooth and square:
And, as I worked, she sat and watched,
Beside me, in her chair.
Night after night, by candlelight,
I cut her lover's name:
Night after night, so still and white,
And like a ghost she came;
And sat beside me in her chair;
And watched with eyes aflame.
She eyed each stroke;
And hardly stirred:
She never spoke
A single word:
And not a sound or murmur broke
The quiet, save the mallet-stroke.
With still eyes ever on my hands,
With eyes that seemed to burn my hands,
My wincing, overwearied hands,
She watched, with bloodless lips apart,
And silent, indrawn breath:
And every stroke my chisel cut,
Death cut still deeper in her heart:
The two of us were chiseling,
Together, I and death.

And when at length the job was done,
And I had laid the mallet by,
As if, at last, her peace were won,
She breathed his name; and, with a sigh,

Passed slowly through the open door:
And never crossed my threshold more.

Next night I labored late, alone.
To cut her name upon the stone.

Wilfrid Wilson Gibson was a prolific writer, turning out more than 30 volumes of verse and drama—yet he never attended school! His work is mainly concerned with the struggle of the common man to get by from day to day. Among his best-known poems are "The Ice Cart," "John Pattison Gibson," "Fires," "Solway Ford," "The Voice," and "The Stone." His major plays are Daily Bread *and* Kestrel Edge.

The Owl-Critic

JAMES T. FIELDS (1817-1881)

"Who stuffed that white owl?" No one spoke in the
    shop,
The barber was busy, and he couldn't stop;
The customers, waiting their turns, were all reading
The *Daily*, the *Herald*, the *Post*, little heeding
The young man who blurted out such a blunt
    question;
Not one raised a head, or even made a suggestion;
    And the barber kept on shaving.

"Don't you see, Mr. Brown,"
Cried the youth, with a frown,
"How wrong the whole thing is,
How preposterous each wing is,
How flattened the head is, how jammed down the
    neck is—

In short, the whole owl, what an ignorant wreck 't is!
I make no apology;
I've learned owl-eology.
I've passed days and nights in a hundred collections,
And cannot be blinded to any deflections
Arising from unskillful fingers that fail
To stuff a bird right, from his beak to his tail.
Mister Brown! Mister Brown!
Do take that bird down,
Or you'll soon be the laughing-stock all over town!"
    And the barber kept on shaving.

"I've *studied* owls,
And other night-fowls,
And I tell you
What I know to be true;
An owl cannot roost
With his limbs so unloosed;
No owl in this world
Ever had his claws curled,
Ever had his legs slanted,
Ever had his bill canted,
Ever had his neck screwed
Into that attitude.
He can't *do* it, because
'Tis against all bird-laws.
Anatomy teaches,
Ornithology preaches,
An owl has a toe
That *can't* turn out so!

I've made the white owl my study for years,
And to see such a job almost moves me to tears!
Mr. Brown, I'm amazed
You should be so gone crazed
As to put up a bird
In that posture absurd!
To *look* at that owl really brings on a dizziness
The man who stuffed *him* don't half know his
    business!"
  And the barber kept on shaving.

"Examine those eyes.
I'm filled with surprise
Taxidermists should pass
Off on you such poor glass;
So unnatural they seem
They'd make Audubon scream,
And John Burroughs laugh
To encounter such chaff.
Do take that bird down;
Have him stuffed again, Brown!"
  And the barber kept on shaving.

"With some sawdust and bark
I could stuff in the dark
An owl better than that.
I could make an old hat
Look more like an owl
Than that horrid fowl,
Stuck up there so stiff like a side of coarse leather.
In fact, about *him*, there's not one natural feather."

Just then, with a wink and a sly normal lurch,
The owl, very gravely, got down from his perch,
Walked around, and regarded his fault-finding critic
(Who thought he was stuffed) with a glance analytic,
And then fairly hooted, as if he should say:
"Your learning's at fault *this* time, anyway;
Don't waste it again on a live bird, I pray.
I'm an owl; you're another. Sir Critic, good day!"
  And the barber kept on shaving.

James Thomas Fields was born in New Hampshire. At the age of sixteen, he came to Boston to make his fortune. Five years later, he was a junior partner in Ticknor & Fields, the most prominent publisher in the city. Among the authors he aided were Longfellow, Holmes, Hawthorne, Emerson, and Lowell. From 1861 to 1872, he served as editor of The Atlantic Monthly.

Fields wrote several volumes of verse and literary reminiscences, among them Yesterdays with Authors *(1872),* Hawthorne *(1876), and* In and Out of Doors with Charles Dickens *(1876). The ground-floor office where Fields labored as publisher is today a Boston landmark.*

Jean Desprez

ROBERT SERVICE (1874-1958)

Oh, ye whose hearts are resonant, and ring to War's
    romance,
Hear ye the story of a boy, a peasant boy of France;
A lad uncouth and warped with toil, yet who, when
    trial came,
Could feel within his soul upleap and soar the sacred
    flame;
Could stand upright, and scorn and smite, as only
    heroes may:
Oh, hearken! Let me try to tell the tale of Jean
    Desprez.

With fire and sword the Teuton horde was ravaging
    the land,
And there was darkness and despair, grim death on
    every hand;
Red fields of slaughter sloping down to ruin's black
    abyss;
The wolves of war ran evil-fanged, and little did they
    miss.
And on they came with fear and flame, to burn and
    loot and slay,
Until they reached the red-roofed croft, the home of
    Jean Desprez.

"Rout out the village, one and all!" the Uhlan Captain
    said.
"Behold! Some hand has fired a shot. My trumpeteer
    is dead.
Now shall they Prussian vengeance know; now shall
    they rue the day,
For by this sacred German slain, ten of these dogs
    shall pay."

They drove the cowering peasants forth, women and
    babies and men,
And from the last, with many a jeer, the Captain
    chose he ten;
Ten simple peasants, bowed with toil; they stood,
    they knew not why,
Against the grey wall of the church, hearing their
    children cry;
Hearing their wives and mothers wail, with faces
    dazed they stood.
A moment only . . . *Ready! Fire!* They weltered in
    their blood.

But there was one who gazed unseen, who heard the
    frenzied cries,
Who saw these men in sabots fall before their
    children's eyes;
A Zouave wounded in a ditch, and knowing death
    was nigh,
He laughed with joy: "Ah! here is where I settle ere I
    die."

He clutched his rifle once again, and long he aimed
    and well. . . .
A shot! Beside his victims ten the Uhlan Captain fell.

They dragged the wounded Zouave out; their rage
    was like a flame.
With bayonets they pinned him down, until their
    Major came.
A blond, full-blooded man he was, and arrogant of
    eye;
He stared to see with shattered skull his favorite
    Captain lie.
"Nay, do not finish him so quick, this foreign swine,"
    he cried;
"Go nail him to the big church door; he shall be
    crucified."

With bayonets through hands and feet they nailed the
    Zouave there,
And there was anguish in his eyes, and horror in his
    stare;
"Water! A single drop!" he moaned; but how they
    jeered at him,
And mocked him with an empty cup, and saw his
    sight grow dim;
And as in agony of death with blood his lips were
    wet,
The Prussian Major gaily laughed, and lit a cigarette.

But mid the white-faced villagers who cowered in
  horror by,
Was one who saw the woeful sight, who heard the
  woeful cry:
"Water! One little drop, I beg! For love of Christ who
  died. . . . "
It was the little Jean Desprez who turned and stole
  aside;
It was the little bare-foot boy who came with cup
  abrim
And walked up to the dying man, and gave the drink
  to him.

A roar of rage! They seize the boy; they tear him fast
  away.
The Prussian Major swings around; no longer is he
  gay.
His teeth are wolfishly agleam; his face all dark with
  spite:
"Go, shoot the brat," he snarls, "that dare defy our
  Prussian might.
Yet stay! I have another thought. I'll kindly be, and
  spare;
Quick; give the lad a rifle charged, and set him
  squarely there,
And bid him shoot, and shoot to kill. Haste! Make
  him understand
The dying dog he fain would save shall perish by his
  hand.

And all his kindred they shall see, and all shall curse
    his name,
Who bought his life at such a cost, the price of death
    and shame."

They brought the boy, wild-eyed with fear; they
    made him understand;
They stood him by the dying man, a rifle in his hand.
"Make haste!" said they; "the time is short, and you
    must kill or die."
The Major puffed his cigarette, amusement in his
    eye.
And then the dying Zouave heard, and raised his
    weary head:
"Shoot, son, 'twill be the best for both; shoot swift
    and straight," he said.
"Fire first and last, and do not flinch; for lost to hope
    am I;
And I will murmur: *Vive La France!* and bless you
    ere I die."

Half-blind with blows the boy stood there; he
    seemed to swoon and sway;
Then in that moment woke the soul of little Jean
    Desprez.
He saw the woods go sheening down; the larks were
    singing clear;
And oh! the scents and sounds of spring, how sweet
    they were! how dear!

He felt the scent of new-mown hay, a soft breeze
    fanned his brow;
O God! the paths of peace and toil! How precious
    were they now!
The summer days and summer ways, how bright
    with hope and bliss!
The autumn such a dream of gold . . . and all must end
    in this:
This shining rifle in his hand, that shambles all
    around;
The Zouave there with dying glare; the blood upon
    the ground;
The brutal faces round him ringed, the evil eyes
    aflame;
That Prussian bully standing by, as if he watched a
    game.
"Make haste and shoot," the Major sneered; "a
    minute more I give;
A minute more to kill your friend, if you yourself
    would live."

They only saw a bare-foot boy, with blanched and
    twitching face;
They did not see within his eyes the glory of his race;
The glory of a million men who for fair France have
    died,
The splendor of self-sacrifice that will not be denied.
Yet . . . he was but a peasant lad, and oh! but life was
    sweet. . . .
"Your minute's nearly gone, my lad," he heard a
    voice repeat.

"Shoot! Shoot!" the dying Zouave moaned; "Shoot! Shoot!" the soldiers said.
Then Jean Desprez reached out and shot . . . *the Prussian Major dead!*

"Jean Desprez" is probably Robert Service's most exciting melodramatic poem. The reader is swept through the verses to the surprising climax, willingly suspending disbelief of the sentimentalized story.

This poem, like "Fleurette," appeared in Rhymes of a Red Cross Man. *Although Service wrote several subsequent books of verse, none attained the popularity of his poems of the Yukon and his war poems. Service's autobiography was published in two volumes—*Ploughman of the Moon *(1945) and* Harper of Heaven *(1948).*

For a biographical note on Service, see page 28.